LEADERSHIP
PLUS

DISCOVER THE LEADER WITHIN

NEERAJ CHANDHOK

INDIA · SINGAPORE · MALAYSIA

Notion Press

Old No. 38, New No. 6
McNichols Road, Chetpet
Chennai - 600 031

First Published by Notion Press 2020
Copyright © Neeraj Chandhok 2020
All Rights Reserved.

ISBN 978-1-64828-894-4

In the loving memory of
Smt. Sushma Devi
(Mother-in-law)

Disclaimer

Although the author has made every effort to ensure that the information in this book was correct at press time, the author and publisher do not assume and hereby disclaim any liability to any party for any loss, damage, or disruption caused by errros or omissions, whether such errors or omissions result from negligence, accident or any other cause.

All the characters in this work are fictional.

Somewhere in busyness and complexities of life we have stopped questioning events and behavior around us. "Discover the leadership within" is an attempt to emphasize on practicing leadership behavior in our personal & professional lives. It is written to inspire and motivate to bring out more leaders. This book is an attempt to encourage questioning and introspection of choices we make. It is about unleashing the leadership behavior not for academic purpose only but for application in our lives, leading to achieving our life purpose! We need to earn our leadership everyday.

Are you being a leader today?

INDEX

FOREWORD

Writing books is an uphill task especially for working professionals as they are time pressed. At the start I wish to congratulate Mr. Chandhok on writing this second book, first one being Customer Plus a customer service strategy book. The Author has been a Corporate Trainer with Chanalai Hotels & Resorts and has made significant contribution assisting and coaching our teams in scaling new heights. To me Leadership is a behavior and the real task of the leader is to develop more leaders. Leadership is complex work, and Mr. Chandhok has succeeded in explaining the essence of leadership through a simple conversation format supported by stories & researches making the topic relevant not only for professionals but also inspiring to the readers to be leaders in personal lives. There is an underlying thread which binds the entire conversation as the conversation moves from personal to organizational and to essence of leadership & leadership behavior.

Leadership is often confused by titles and positions in business environment however it is all about behavior. Leadership has to be trust based and purpose driven.

"I believe that Leadership is about leaders sharing their belief, vision and passion with teams and in the process they inspire others to believe. Belief creates high confidence and commitment on the journey and leaders are positively contagious"

Ambar Mazumdar
CEO-Chanalai Hotels & Resorts
Phuket Thailand

LEADERSHIP PLUS- DISCOVER THE LEADER WITHIN

Leaders come in many roles and are present all around us, could be a teacher, a nurse, a doctor or a fire fighter, a single parent, our parents, business owner, someone in a corporate position, a soldier, someone serving society, someone fighting a serious disease with fortitude or may be a student studying or someone pursuing his dream against all odds.

Since I have been a teacher and a keen learner, this book has taken the shape of a teacher and student discussion. This book is based on a conversation format between Nick & Roy. They both represent me in two roles. Nick is the one who is inquisitive about learning more about how to lead, develop leadership skills and curious to learn more about re-inventing self.

And Roy is that courage and inner voice which fuels growth by investing long hours to answer Nick's queries. These two got committed to engage on a path to discover and strengthen the leader within to learn about the essence of leadership that one could apply in personal and professional life.

The content is about a journey of discovering the leadership within each one of us. How developing leadership behavior is essential to succeed both personally and professionally. The journey unfolds path to success and leading effectively.

It also aims to be used as a tool to learn and interpret leadership and its importance. The journey discovers blind spots that we may have about leadership and attempts to mirror out those.

ACKNOWLEDGEMENT

Thank you Dear Mom Dad for your guidance & inspiration.

Heartfelt gratitude to the following, without them this Book would not have been possible. I sincerely express my gratitude to all the leaders I got an opportunity to work with, all my teachers, my friends, & students who inspired me to keep pace with the changing and challenging work.

Thank you Dr. R. K. Gupta, Mr. Ambar Mazumdar & Mr. Munish Vasudeva & for engaging in discussions on leadership

I would like to express my thanks and gratitude to the following for capturing various ideation and converting them into amazing illustrations.

Mr. Lovneet Singh (Bobby),

Ms. Chandrokala Biswas (Chandro),

Abhishek Verma,

Himanshu Kaushal,

Editor: Mr. Harjot Singh

Thank you Harjot Singh for patiently editing the script

Thank you for patiently reviewing the content and for your suggestions.

A big thank you to my students Archit Gupta & Mallhar Mohapatra & Ms. Mandeep Kaur for their valuable assistance. Thank You Ms. Sneha Ann. Last but not the least this book would not have been possible without the incredible support of the publishing manager Ms. Sneha Ann of Notion Press. Ms. Sneha your professional attitude with your customers is an inspiring example to excel. You are a leader!

This book would not have been possible without the support of my family & friends. Thank you, Ms Mona Vij, Mr. Vijay Gupta, Mr. Vivek Sahney & Mr. Vikas Pal.

Respected Mr. M. Z. Khan, we are truly blessed to have your blessings and your guidance and life lessons

THE ART OF TRANSFORMING VISION INTO REALITY

"You are never given a dream without also being given the power to make it true. You may have to work for it, however."

– Richard Bach

Richard David Bach is an American writer & is widely known as the author of some of the 1970s' biggest sellers, including Jonathan Livingston Seagull (1970) and Illusions

Nick: Questions about leadership have always intrigued me since childhood, but the topic has so many interpretations that it makes its understanding extremely complex.

Roy: It is a complex subject for sure and the entrepreneurs and leaders are so pushed to achieve results faster that leadership is often compromised for personal gains and also confused with aiming for short term profits & not targeting for long term success.

Nick: Some of the leadership questions that I have always wanted answers for are?

- What is the essence of leadership?

- How can one be a leader in personal and professional life?

- What makes a truly effective leader?

- Why people follow someone?

- How leadership influences one's personal & professional life?

- How can leadership be the key to one's success?

- Why some people succeed and others don't?

Roy: You have raised certain expectations which require us to engage together on a journey to discover the secrets of leadership

Let's Begin the journey and see what unfolds!!

Nick: I will start by sharing some definitions!!

Leadership consists of five fundamental practices that enable leaders to get extraordinary things accomplished: model the way, inspire a shared vision, challenge the process, enable others to act and encourage the heart.

– (Kouzes & Poster 2002)

Leadership is a process whereby an individual influences a group of individuals to achieve a common goal.

– (Northouse 2007)

Nick: This journey of Leadership learning is what I have missed in my education and as I brain storm, I am beginning to understand how crucial it is in our lives to achieve our goals.

Roy: I completely agree with you. In a lot of ways, leaders are like magicians, that is why they are viewed in awe by their followers. They are those who have a vision of future and commit themselves to transform them into reality.

And when they are able to convert their vision into reality, people watch in disbelief and wonder how did they achieve that? The goal almost looked unachievable when it was started.

Leaders have stronger imagination than those who have only knowledge. Knowledge is limited however imagination has no restrictions. In a way leaders can visualize their imagination coming true, but those with only knowledge have a limitation. However just having a vision is not enough it must be supported by execution to turn it into reality.

Nick: Allow me to share the quote by Arnold Schwarzenegger

"If you want to turn a vision into reality, you have to give 100% and never stop believing in your dream."

Arnold is an Austrian-American actor, filmmaker, businessman, author, and former professional bodybuilder and politician. Won Mr. Olympia contest seven times

Who could imagine that in the smart phone industry customers would buy an iPhone for such an exorbitant price? This was unheard of in the market but someone did imagine and created one of the most valued brands in the world – Apple!

Who could imagine that a coffee chain could have 27000+ outlets in the world, in more than 70 countries but Howard Schultz did dream and created world's largest coffee house company in the world. Starbucks!!

Who could imagine that there is a possibility of creating a business out of reused rockets and sending them to again to space but Elon Musk could, and his company Space X created history by doing that.

It is almost impossible to have won 28 medals in Olympics which Michael Phelps has to his credit as the most legendary swimmer.

Nick: Michael Phelps medals tally if measured against the countries olympics achievement, Michael personal achievements would place him amongst top 50 countries.

Michael Phelps (Retired American swimmer & most successful and most decorated Olympian of all time, with a total of 28 medals. Phelps also holds the all-time records for highest Olympic gold medals)

Nick: All these achievements seem like a miracle.

Roy: It is a miracle but it comes true with belief, faith, focus and lot of hard work. That is why it is achieved by only a handful of people and not by everyone.

Nick: Do you mean leader's fuel their belief and faith and not their fears!

Roy: That is why it is said 365 times in bible "do not be afraid" one for every day.

Nick: And also it mentions faith can move mountains! So let us begin with faith and belief and not to be fearful and afraid as a start point of leadership.

Nick: Why is it that only very little percentage of people is able to succeed in their ambition?

"Opportunity is missed by most people because it is dressed in overalls and looks like hard work."

– Thomas Edison

Roy: We all want to achieve various goals in our lives but only a small percentage of us are able to live a life of choice & to make a choice one has to be decisive. We must choose and take a decision and then make a plan and move ahead. Being indecisive is a costly mistake. Life changes completely when we are decisive and committed to a cause.

"Life changes the moment you make a new congruent and committed decision."

– Anthony Robbins

Anthony Jay Robbins is an American author, philanthropist, and life coach.

LEADERS MUST BE DECISIVE

"Indecision is the thief of opportunity."

– Jim Rohn

Emanuel James Rohn professionally known as Jim Rohn, was an American entrepreneur, author and motivational speaker.

Roy: Not taking decision is a drawback and the underlying cause of that could be fear, poor habits, lack of courage, lack of taking initiative, lack of self-belief, or may be as simple as being lazy or may be too happy to stay in one's comfort zone.

Nick: But isn't decision making complex business as one has too many options?

Roy: Yes & it is getting more and more complex as the number of options and choices before us are increasing! FOBO (fear of better option) with the availability of abundant information we tend to keep postponing the decision as we constantly feel we may find something better and more suitable.

Roy: I am sure this one helps?

"In any moment of decision, the best thing you can do is the right thing, the next best thing is the wrong thing, and the worst thing you can do is nothing"

– Theodore Roosevelt

(Theodore Roosevelt Jr. was an American statesman, politician, conservationist, naturalist, and writer who served as the 26th president of the United States from 1901 to 1909.)

Nick: It does! I understand that a decision and acting upon it, is certainly better than taking no decision at all. Delayed decisions can cost a lot hence leadership must be active and agile.

Roy: Leaders must be decisive. Being un-decisive can be more harmful than taking a wrong decision. Wrong decisions still keep things moving and can be corrected but taking no decisions brings an organization to a standstill. This may lead to loss of reputation which may take years to recover from.

Leaders, in order to be decisive must be:

Able to work under ambiguous situations which are not crystal clear and hence they must adapt and stay agile

They should be able to see opportunities during uncertainties.

Nick: And over and above that they have time pressures to complete projects but I am sure the detailed data available to them makes their decision making easy. Oops did I forget the FOBO! (Fear of better option)

Roy: In spite of all the data available, there is always some missing link which requires a decision. Leaders must decide to take a direction out of many options available & stay accountable for the consequences of their decision. Data is mostly supportive in providing directional approach, it is like a brief plot but the story needs to be built by the leader depending on his forecasting qualities.

In short by being decisive, leaders actually choose between acting and not acting, they know that in spite of all the knowledge there are still going to be lot of variable along the way.

Nick: So no matter how much preparation is made there will still be variations to that during execution. Not everything can be controlled

Roy: Leaders must act and should not get struck in over-planning and over analyzing. Over planning is sometimes a result of being scared! In-spite of the best of the business plans created, leaders know that it's a plan at the end of the day and execution is going to be different than that!

PLAN

LOOKS SIMPLE EXECUTION IS COMPLEX

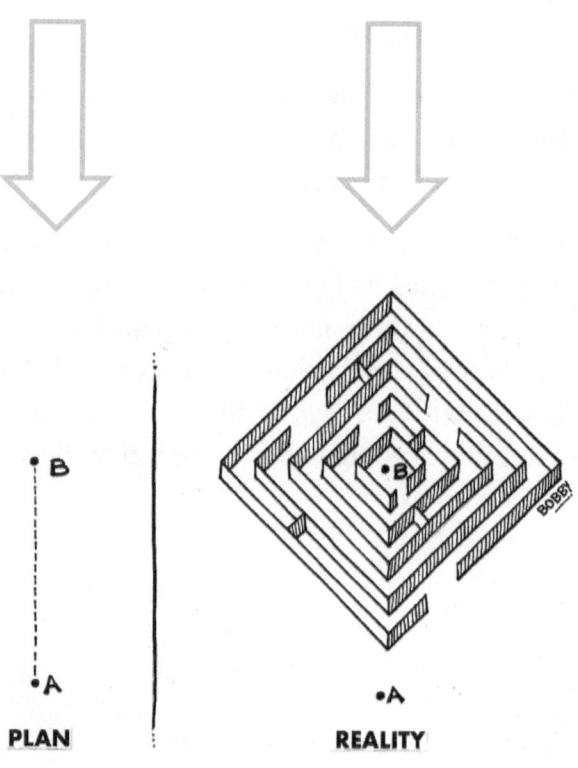

How a plan looks like How a Plan Works-Out

In the Beginning When Executed

LEADERS MUST BE DARING

"You miss 100% of the shots you don't take"

Wayne Gretzky: is a Canadian former professional ice hockey player and former head coach, often called as" the greatest hockey player ever" by many sportswriters and players.

Roy: Leaders are daring individuals and take risks.

We cannot make much progress if we keep focusing about what all can go wrong! It is the fear of risk not actually the real risk. Leaders understand that risking something and failing will not be the end their efforts. Leaders must embrace risk as part of their life as compared to those who have never taken risks have not tasted failure as well and would have never made a comeback too. Those always sitting safely over previous achievements would not know much about how to handle a set back or a failure. Those who don't risk also shows that they don't take initiative as well, which means they are happy being at the status quo and sitting under the glory of past achievements.

Risk taking is essential to tap into new and future opportunities.

Nick: Are you saying that there is huge risk in not taking risk?

Roy: In a book titled Empires of the Mind author Denis Waitley makes a reference and makes a point about the risk of not taking a risk. The author has mentioned a tribe in Amazon in South America who were inflicted by a certain unknown disease and many deaths occurred because of that. Some physicians got friendly with the tribe and identified the reason for the disease. The reason was an insect that was on the walls of their houses. These physicians offered them three options: they could allow doctors to spray medicines on the walls of their house, they could make new houses at another place or do nothing and continue to live the same way. To utter surprise the tribe choose the last option i.e. to continue living the same way.

It seems like we embrace our fear and limitation and don't let them go and don't take risk feeling comfortable embracing our fears believing change would be even worse. This is one of the key reasons why many people fail to develop their full potential.

Nick: And stay prisoners to our own fears and limitations.

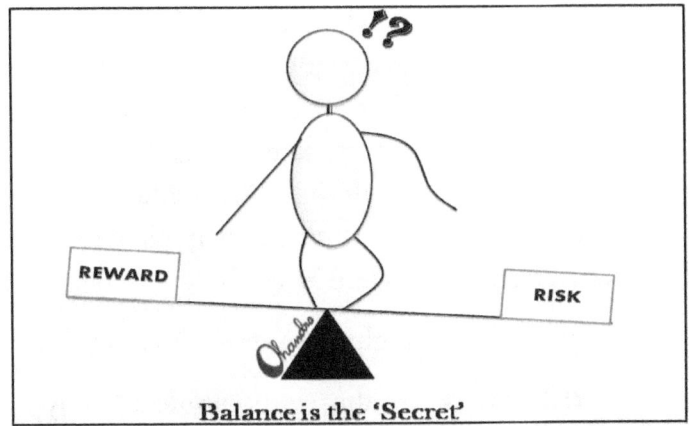
Balance is the 'Secret'

Nick: Risk as defined by Merriam-Webster's dictionary is a: possibility of loss or injury, *by* someone or something that creates or suggests a hazard.

Nick: Risk taking is attempting or undertaking a task where the outcome of the efforts is not certain

Roy: Or when there is a possibility of facing a failure!

Nick: Let us see what happens if we don't take any risks?

Our results become predictable & our achievements are also not substantial.

Why most of us shirk away from risk taking?

Roy: At the core of not taking any risks is fear! Progress is what keeps the humanity going. And all the progress is made by those who believed that there is a way to create a better future and hence they try to take a new path and take an initiative. As a matter of fact more than often not taking risk has worse consequences than taking risks. Also remember risks also give disproportionate results. To achieve bigger rewards one must risk or one may have to settle for average results and rewards.

Let me also highlight the types of risk takers

- **Risk takers:** are those who are excited by an opportunity which involves risk and often jump too quickly without assessing the situation

- **Risk Averters:** Are those who plan, plan and plan and never take a plunge. They are struck by over planning and never execute a risk opportunity.

    The idea is to strike a balance between these two!

Roy: To understand this better we may learn from Kahneman & Tversky, 1979) (Daniel Kahneman is a psychologist well-known for his contributions to behavioural economics. He was awarded the Nobel Memorial Prize in Economic Sciences in 2002.

    Amos Nathan Tversky was a cognitive and mathematical psychologist, a student of cognitive science, a collaborator of Daniel

Kahneman, and a figure in the discovery of systematic human cognitive bias and handling of risk.)

"losses loom larger than gains" (Kahneman & Tversky, 1979). Whereby it describes that the psychologically pain of losing is about twice as powerful as the pleasure of gaining"

"the aggravation that one experiences in losing a sum of money appears to be greater than the pleasure associated with gaining the same amount" (Kahneman & Tversky, 1979; p. 279).

That simply means that we associate more pain to losing $10 then we associate pleasure at gaining $10 even though the value of loss and profit is the same.

A study was conducted by Kahneman & Tversky whereby 600 participants were told about a hypothetical disease outbreak in asia threatening to kill 600 people. The participants were given two options to choose from:

Framing	Treatment A	Treatment B
Positive	"Saving = 200 lives"	"A 33% chance of saving all 600 people, 66% possibility of saving no one."
Negative	"400 people will die"	"A 33% chance that no people will die, 66% probability that all 600 will die."

Treatment A was chosen by 72% of participants when it was presented with positive framing ("saves 200 lives") dropping to 22% when the same choice was presented with negative framing ("400 people will die").

People are more willing to take risks (or behave dishonestly; e.g. Schindler & Pfattheicher, 2016) to avoid a loss than to make a gain.

Risk taking is an art, which involves preparation and testing of waters being an essential part of leadership.

Nick: What is testing waters?

Roy: I meant risk a little first and then move to bigger risks! It refers to taking calculated risks. Risk taking leads to being in an uncomfortable situation, may be painful & that leads to adaptation and that is how leaders grow. Leaders analyze, plan and execute. In a way they know there risk taking capacity and take calculated risks. You see fear plays a major role in risks. Over fearing a situation than what it really is makes the risk look bigger however feeling lesser fear, than what it is makes one fearless which is also a misleading picture. Hence leaders must weigh fear and understand its consequences well to be able to deal with that. They must see the situation as it is, neither worse than what it is, nor better than what it is. And then see what all can be done to make it better.

Nick: You mean all those who took risk from a regular path and accepted life challenges could achieve more than those who never took risks!

Roy: Yes that is true. Often we are tempted by the status quo comfort and daily routine which keeps us away from discovering or experimenting anything new in our lives.

Also the society and peers are busy in tuning and training everyone to become part of a process or system leaving little encouragement for innovation.

Nick: And the new path is taken by those who take risks and show resolve to stick by their chosen path

Roy: It is because of such people that the development, inventions and progress of the mankind has taken place, because they took the path less traveled, knowing well that success was not ensured and the path was filled with risks and road-blocks which test their faith and abilities!

Nick: Often in life, I have chosen a safe path! Or sometime felt that I do not know enough to take a new path! How is it that a leader knows everything prior to undertaking an endeavor?

Roy: No amount of analysis can ensure future success of an endeavor. Leaders do the following:

> They trust their instinct
>
> They know making mistakes is a part of success, so they don't refrain from starting just because they fear failure.
>
> They avoid the paralysis of analysis trap by over thinking
>
> And a leader must think out of the box and adapt to navigate through risk which is a new path. Leaders do things which have not been done before, but with a trusted team they overcome the obstacles.

If you are not willing to risk the unusual, you will have to settle for the ordinary.

– Jim Rohn

Roy: Leaders know that they don't know all the answers but believe to cross the river when it comes!

Nick: Can you please explain this a little more?

Roy: While climbing a mountain the mountaineer cannot see all the peaks that he will be scaling! The best he can do is to plan and prepare for the expedition. Let us consider a risk taking expedition of climbing moutains. Once the first peak is reached the team sees the other side of the mountain. Inspite of the best of preparation and taking calculated risk, there is always a risk involved. The next peak is visible only after climbing the first one and so on let me explain with an example

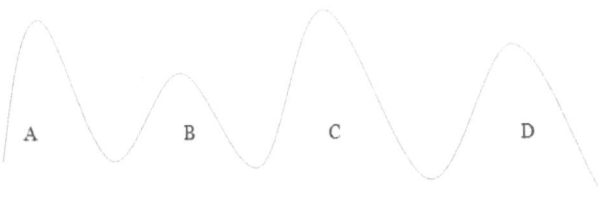

Once peak A is climbed then only B is visible and after climbing B, peak C is visible and the obstacles surface.

Nick: You mean one can only plan, practice and prepare for a challenges at the start but there are bound to be some surprises and obstacles on the way! One can never know all the hurdles and problems in advance that would come on the way while pursuing a challenging vision.

Hence a leader is guided more by courage, grit, self-confidence and belief!!

Roy: It is precisely that. I can't miss the phrase Leap of Faith here, which is simply admitting that we accept the risk of failure. In any leadership and success there is always a possibility of failure, it is a step one takes inspite of knowing the possible failure. It is moving in a direction which has no evidence of success and can't be proved, yet it seems a possibility and one believes in it. By giving our 100% to this effort we can succeed but with a shaky and indecisive mindset no venture can come true. Leaders have that unflinching faith in themselves and the vision they have set their mind to.

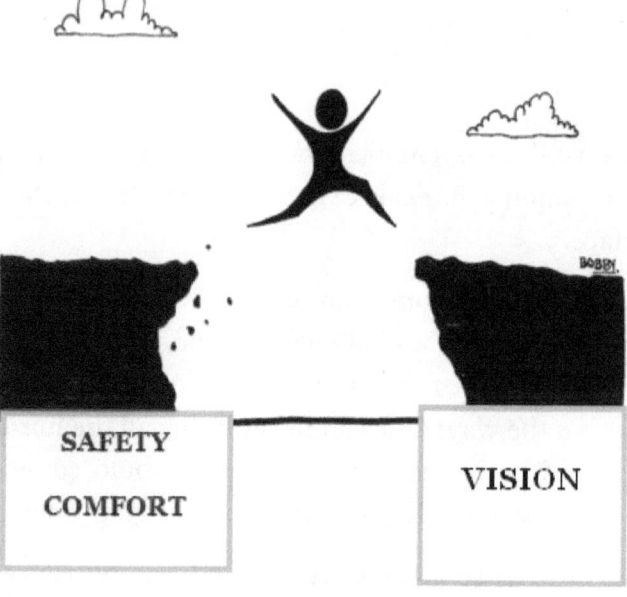

SAFETY

COMFORT

VISION

LEAP OF FAITH

Nick: It is about that belief in oneself to convert an idea or dream into reality.

Roy: Leaders continuously take this leap of faith for example: while hiring a new employee, while promoting someone for a new senior role, taking decision to start a new venture, working to design a new business venture, delegating and trusting a crucial assignment to a colleague.

Nick: It could be promoting a business disruptive idea and committing resources to it etc

Roy: Absolutely.

Nick: I cannot stop from sharing a poem by Robert Frost: "The Road Not Taken"!!

Roy: "Road Not Taken" is all about making choices at the cross roads in life. The essence of the poem is all about how making some choices in life can shape our lives differently.

The poem is symbolic of how we make choices in life. We often choose easy paths and the "road less travelled" is that path which we missed thinking that it is difficult path and may be full of unknown obstacles.

It reflects on the fact that when we are presented with options we must chose and make a decision wisely without getting scared.

It is about contemplation before making a choice.

It is about the road we choose, the choices that we make that designs our life.

Nick: Once decision is made, a plan must be made to achieve that.

Roy: Once a goal is set or a decision is made, starts the complex part, as no one can predict the future variables however, certain traits can be instrumental in reaching the goals

"There is a huge difference between:

1. Just having a goal

    &

2. Executing a Goal with a Plan

An idiot with a plan can beat a genius without a plan."

– **Warren Buffet**

(Warren Edward Buffett is an American business magnate, investor, speaker and philanthropist who served as the chairman and CEO of Berkshire Hathaway)

Mostly people wish, what they hope, someday will get fulfilled on its own. But it is only foolish to expect fruits from a tree when we have not even planted a seed. They keep doing what they have been always doing and expect results to change.

Often people stay as dabblers in various areas without succeeding in any endeavor! A dabbler keeps changing his vision and goals regularly leaving him with little results as he lacks focused effort in the direction of the vision.

Nick: Definition of Dabbler by Merriam-Webster:

"Means a person who follows a pursuit without attaining proficiency or professional status"

Roy: Expecting results without supporting efforts is a sure recipe to depression and failure.

Leaders, like everyone, have a thought, an idea or a goal that they wish to turn to reality. But the difference is that they commit themselves to that idea/concept to see it happen in spite of:

- The fears

- The failures

- The Obstacles

- The Naysayers

- The Competition &

- The Adversaries

- The Criticism

- The Limitations

Nick: Are you trying to say that they seize the power of Decision making and stay committed to that?

Roy: Yes, they are decisive and confidently make a choice and make a firm decision & commit themselves to that.

Nick: And the others are not decisive enough and never make a choice!

Roy: Being decisive is followed up by taking continuous action towards the goal for a considerable amount of time without any loss of enthusiasm.

We all have great ideas but the difference is to commit resources of time energy, capital & efforts to execute that idea. Not only resources but emotional commitment also has to be there.

Nick: And on the other hand others think and think but never commit. Over thinking and over analyzing supported by procrastination leads to paralysis of analysis. (Paralysis of analysis is a situation that develops as a result of over thinking, too much pondering which results in no action)

Some of the reasons that lead to lower productivity are:

- Lacking clarity of vision
- Too many Interruptions
- Not assigning work priority
- Micro-managing people
- Not delegating or reluctance to delegate
- Smart Phones
- Social media addiction
- E-mails
- Work space clutter
- Noisy environment
- Multi-tasking
- Decision fatigue (it's the deteriorating quality of decision making when one has been exposed to, too many decisions within a stipulated time)
- Stress & Anxiety
- Lack of energy due to health reasons
- Checking social media platforms repeatedly as an addiction

The above are some of the work distractions or habits we indulge in which keeps the productivity lower.

Nick: How can we avoid the trap of low productivity?

Roy: Why not use Eisenhower Matrix

Eisenhower was the 34th President of United States, before that he was the General of the United States Army and was also the Allied Forces Supreme Commander during the World War II. His position was extremely demanding and he had to make many important decisions every day. This is when he invented the Eisenhower Matrix of decision making to help prioritize by importance and urgency.

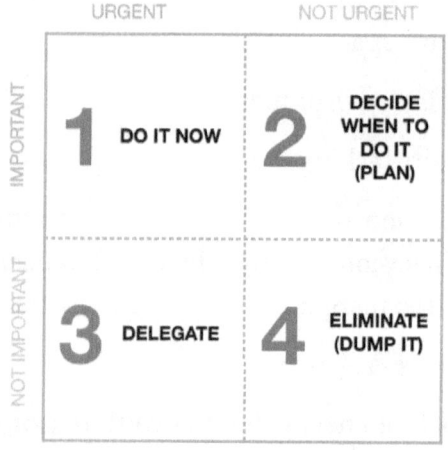

EISENHOVER MATRIX

The most effective and productive leaders spent most of their time in quadrant 2. Which helps them exercise control over the situation

Nick: If they spend more time in other quadrants they would simply be reacting to situations leaving them with no time left with them to do important things.

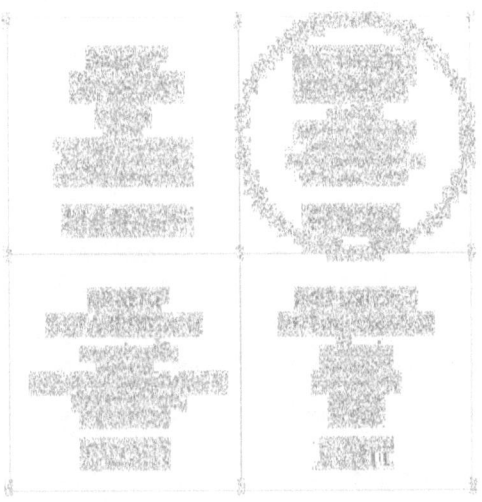

Nick: This is aptly quoted by Lao Tsu:

"Do difficult things when they are easy and do great things when they are small. A journey of 1000 steps must begin with a single step"

LEADERS SAY "NO" TO WASTEFUL STRETCH

The difference between successful people and really successful people is that really successful people say no to almost everything."

– "Warren Buffet"

Roy: To be effective towards a vision, one has to know the power of "No"! Saying No is actually an art. To commit time and energy to one target, one has to block all distractions which are meaningless & do not promote the achievement of the objective. Leaders know the power of saying "NO."

They know the most precious resource that they have is time so they use 'NO' often and stay on course to being productive and not wasting time on unproductive activities. They know that the power of "No" is much underrated. Saying 'NO' signifies that you are clear about what you want and what you don't! They say 'NO' to protect themselves from being robbed of their enthusiasm. By saying 'NO' they stay away from being exploited to commit to un-important tasks; however on the other hand saying 'YES' to most of the things leads to over commitment and stress. Saying

'NO' clearly marks boundaries for others to what is not acceptable

Saying "No" should not be misunderstood, it refers to saying YES to doing things that are relevant to one's objective and tasks and saying "No" to all the tasks and activities that deviate one from the objective.

Nick: It means saying "NO" to all the wasteful activities which delay the objective or which do not contribute in achieving the task.

Roy: True, it refers to having a "To Do List" and at the same time identifying a "Not to Do list" or Stop Doing List which is a list of wasteful activities. Like addiction to social media & unnecessary gossips etc.

Nick: Do you also mean it set boundaries and protects them from any exploitation?

Roy: Completely! Leaders are not in people pleasing business!

By saying 'NO' leaders bring more control to their life and objectives.

They say 'No' to negative influences

They say 'No' to those who pull their spirits and confidence down

Nick: It also saves them from over committing themselves and getting them negatively influenced.

Roy: It is also their duty to protect their team from the negative influence of those who pull the moral of the team down.

Nick: There is always a continuous stream of disturbances and interruptions in our lives!

Roy: There are some techniques to achieve better focus and productivity, which in short, aims at doing few things in a planned manner to excel:

- Keep focus on their goals at all times and never lose sight of the bigger picture.

- Have a simplified understanding of what are the key objectives to be achieved.

- Have a plan for the day: run the day or the day will run you down.

- Manage energies effectively and not let them drain.

- Work on one thing at a time.

- Turning off WhatsApp/e-mails/social media etc. to ensure uninterrupted focus.

- They focus on what to do list?

- They create and also focus on "what to stop doing list"

- Stay extremely aggressive about guarding their time as leaders and know that it is the most important resource.

Nick: I hope that helps in improving my attention span and staying productive.

Roy: Come on Nick, you are highly productive and energetic most of the time, but I agree there is always a scope to get better for all of us.

Nick: I am not sure that I have understood that really well.

Help me understand this. What makes leaders so sure, of their idea that it will work which gives them so much confidence to be decisive? Do they research well or they too much fact finding; I mean how and where does this level of confidence and decisiveness come from?

Roy: That is a brilliant question. There is in fact no guarantee of any endeavor to succeed when you start. Hence there is always a certain amount of risk involved in that! However leaders take that risk and move ahead confidently. However they reduce/control that risk by having more knowledge about the industry or field they plan to work in. They seek more information, train themselves more and equip themselves in taking a decision which helps them in controlling the risk to some extent.

Nick: What would you mean by a controlled risk?

Roy: Certain amount of risk is always there in execution of any endeavor, however leaders reduce that by preparation and knowing more about the situation.

Nick: Got that, it is said in Rome:

As The Spartan warrior said

"Sweat more in training & bleed less in War"

– Anonymous

Are leaders prepared to take path breaking decisions & path breakings risks and see them through till they succeed?

Roy: I have always loved the famous quote from Mr. Ratan Tata:

"I don't believe in taking right decisions, I take decisions and then make them

– "Ratan Tata"

(Padma Vibhushan, Padma Bhushan) (Ratan Naval Tata is an Indian industrialist, investor, and philanthropist)

Nick: I know what you are trying to say, is that in spite of the best of preparation, taking a new path is always risky! There will always be some or the other variations to the original plan. So leaders must be mentally, physically and emotionally equipped as well as committed to handle constantly changing environment. They must be able to adapt to change and stay agile and not rigid.

Roy: By rigid it means that what got us here will also help us stay ahead always. This kind of rigid thinking could lead to disaster

Nick: Like in west they say: don't fix it, if it is not broken?

Roy: And in Japan they say, fix it even its not broken, which means we can keep improving even if no one is complaining.

Nick: You mean, to keep improving continuously & not get complacent. Leaders should never stay in a spot where they stop questioning themselves about how they can contribute or serve better.

Does that reflect that leaders continuously have to learn, unlearn and re-learn.

Roy: The speed at which the world is changing, the challenge is to always keep learning, adapt to changes and be able to reinvent oneself.

LEADERS TAKE BIG POWERFUL ACTION

"Vision without execution is hallucination."

– Thomas Edison

PURPOSE OF KNOWING IS TO DO

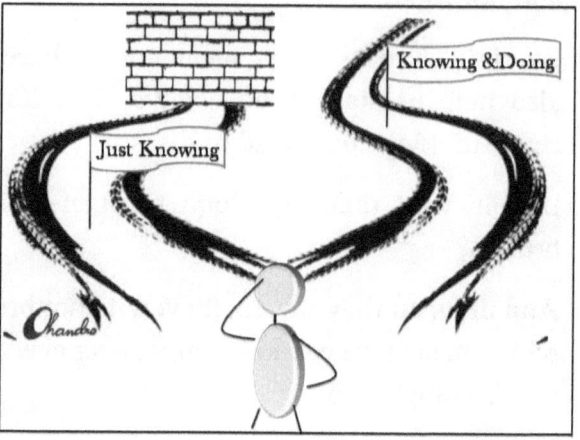

"Inaction breeds doubt and fear. Action breeds confidence and courage. If you want to conquer fear, do not sit home and think about it. Go out and get busy."

– Dale Carnegie

(Dale Breckenridge Carnegie was an American writer and lecturer)

Roy: The execution of the idea is everything. Having just an idea is of no value until it's executed successfully which requires courage and grit.

Knowing is important but doing is the real thing. Having an idea is not important, execution of the idea is!

Nick: What do you mean by taking big action?

Roy: One of the key qualities of leaders is to influence others to take action but before inspiring others to do so it is important that they know clearly what action taking route looks like.

Taking big decisive action is essential to accomplishing any endeavor! Leaders believe in taking action towards their goals for a considerable period of time and take complete responsibility for the same. They always carry the bigger picture in their mind, about what is to be accomplished and ensure that the actions are driven towards that at all times.

Lack of taking action leads to fear and doubts, however taking big action adds to confidence and courage.

Nick: How is taking action different than taking big action?

Roy: Taking action would mean that some action is being taken towards the goals or aspirations however big action is different from that. It means the presence of the following elements:

- Focused action towards the goals and the priorities

- Consistent Action towards the goals

- Having teams aligned and motivated with the vision

- Action towards the goals for a considerably long period to show results

- Taking responsibility towards the outcomes of the efforts

Nick: I understand what you mean! It is somewhat like preparation done by Champions in sports, such as these:

- They practice consistently and religiously for a considerable period of time

- They remain focused towards developing their skills/game in various aspects

- They prepare themselves physically, mentally and emotionally for the highest possible levels &

- The champions also tend to practice more than their competitors

As Mohammad Ali has said:

"I don't count my sit-ups; I only start counting when it starts hurting because they're the only ones that count."

– **Mohammad Ali**

Nick: The quote somehow shows the mindset of the winners, they are not in a game just for the sake of it. But they are in it to win and they commit to work hard, plan, prepare and sacrifice for the same. Their commitment to an objective is well backed by their emotional, physical and mental strength, to achieve more.

Roy: Similarly leaders once they have locked in a target, they commit to taking big action in its direction continuously. They may change their route to the goal though.

In the absence of any action all dreams remain unfulfilled and there is nothing more tragic in a life than the feeling of regret of not having done things which we all wanted to accomplish in our lives.

Nick: You mean The cost of regret is much more than the cost of action and its consequences!

Roy: Very right! Consistent action creates habits which further yield more accomplishments. Consistent action towards a goal helps eliminate what does not work and creates path for more innovation that ultimately yields success.

"Action is the foundational key to all success."

– Pablo Picasso

Pablo Ruiz Picasso was a Spanish painter, sculptor, printmaker, ceramicist, stage designer, poet and playwright

Without actions all plans and dreams remain only dreams. Without action no dreams come true. It is not only about having a great plan but also an excellent execution that leads to results.

Nick: That makes me feel that all effective leaders should also be excellent at executing the plan.

Roy: Very true, they have to be extremely skilled Managers as well.

Roy: However leadership is an extremely complex role. No wonder leadership change plays a crucial role in organizations.

Nick: What role does a leader play?

Roy: A Leader should be effective across levels:

1. Personal Leadership: He should be decisive, trust worthy, self-motivated, goal oriented, productive and driven by values.

2. Professional Leadership: Clearly communicates the vision, inspires, connects and engages the team with the organizational goals, is decisive and takes ownership of the outcomes, instills confidence in the team to succeed, avoids micro managing, empowers teams, creates a people first work culture, Walk the talk, develops and coaches teams leading to empowered teams, shares credit for achievements.

   Practices flexibility and rigidity as per the situation, governed by fairness and organizational values.

3. Influence: At this level one should display empathy, fairness, be a good listener, encouraging and objective, walk the talk approach by keeping his/her word and promises.

4. Ability to take big action: Drives the organization and team to execute massive action plans consistently with confidence.

Nick: That is great dissection of his role, gives me clarity about what leadership is about. It is actually a behavior and not a position or a title.

Roy: Very right Nick, you have just stated the Essence of the Leadership

Nick: Why is it that leaders are decisive and feel confident of committing themselves to goals/ vision even in the face of adversity and unknown fears?

Roy: This is how it works!

First to have a compelling vision, and then to have a plan to achieve it

Leaders have clarity of their objective by visualizing in detail how their success would look like before they start executing it. This visualization fueled by passion to succeed keeps them going. All goals are first visualized in mind before they become a reality.

LEADERS MUST BE PRAGMATIC & NOT DOGMATIC IN APPROACH

Roy: Leaders achieve practical solutions in a real world. Pragmatic leaders are practical thinkers and they give a lot of importance to the process behind a task. They try to view how their team is going to complete the task at hand. They are not simply stuck or dependent upon theoretical aspect of situation or scientific research based decision approach only. Applying pragmatic approach is to solve problems in a sensible manner, keeping in view the realistic conditions. This approach is much more effective in achieving a solution as it requires staying flexible and thinking innovative ways of decision making rather than only applying policies, procedures and guidelines

Nick: Pragmatic means living in the real world and not in a perfect world.

Roy: Dogmatic is when someone is living in a world that one wants to be in and feels and behaves a little stuck up. One always wants to work within certain rules and framework and finds it difficult to adapt. A dogmatic leader will follow rules no matter what. They are always rigid towards people, and have a rigid approach towards problem solving too, which restricts them majorly in their progress.

Nick: Must confess sometimes I get stuck up because of my ego!

Roy: We will tackle that as well as we move ahead.

Nick: This seems to be more a journey of self-discovery as I am able to see many blind spots, in my personality, which I need to improve upon.

I sometimes feel that I am the biggest hindrance to my own progress.

I feel sometimes I lack courage or may be grit?

Roy: Let us try and learn a little more about courage!!

Nick: How is grit different from courage?

Roy: Grit is about showing and facing situations with courage consistently. It is like rising up to the situation or problems with persistence each time.

Nick: I would want to explore more about courage and grit!

COURAGE-THE ESSENTIAL QUALITY TO LEAD

"Courage is the first of human qualities because it is the quality which guarantees the others."

– Aristotle

(Aristotle was a Greek philosopher, Along with his teacher Plato, he has been called the "Father of Western Philosophy")

Roy: The word courage is derived from the Medieval Old French term corage, meaning "heart and spirit."

Courage is that quality which enables a person to face danger, pain, painful situations, trying and difficult times without being fearful.

Nick: What makes courage so important in Leadership?

Roy: Without courage there cannot be any leadership. Courage is important because the speed at which things are changing, we are extremely uncertain how things will turn out in the coming few years. Mind loves certainty and not ambiguity. Being in a fearful unknown situation can be extremely uncomfortable but working through that shapes the leaders.

Nick: Is courage about standing up and speaking up for what you believe in face of adversity?

Roy: It is also about accepting that one does not know everything, it is about making mistakes, it is also about, to sit and listen attentively, it is about keeping teams morale and motivation high during troubled times.

Nick: Is there a connection between courage and self-confidence?

Roy: Self-confidence is the courage to know self and about self-image. We all have an image of ourselves in our mind. It could be a real picture or may be ideal picture of ourselves. In short it is trust in one's abilities, competency, qualities and one's judgement.

- Self-confidence is about belief in yourself

- Valuing yourself for who you are

- Standing up for your beliefs & being assertive

- Taking action based on your beliefs

- Feeling good about yourself

- Feeling worthy of respect, love and friendship

Nick: "Self-confidence can be described as an ability to be certain about one's competencies and skills. It includes a sense of self-esteem and self-assurance and the belief that one can make a difference" (Northhouse, 2007, p.20).

It is essential that leaders must be confident as it is natural that confident people are presumed to be competent as well because of this people easily follow and trust them, In the absence of confidence leaders cannot make decisions. Confidence leads to conviction and if leaders are unsure of themselves & their decisions they fail to inspire. Leaders must have self-belief as they lead the teams to unsure paths and unknown future ahead.

Hence no leadership is possible in the absence of self confidence

Roy: Courage is the foundation of leadership because:

- It takes courage to withstand a Conflict & Resolve

- It takes courage to take a Risk!

- It takes courage to venture on a new challenging new path!

- It takes courage to Trust!

- It takes courage to say "No"!

- It takes courage to Disagree!

- It takes courage to take Bold & Unpopular Decisions

- It takes courage to share credit and give credit

- It takes courage to Talk Straight!

- It takes courage to accept a Mistake!

- It takes courage to say I need to know this or I do not know this!

- It takes courage to disturb or upset the Status Quo!

- It takes courage to stay accountable or accept Responsibility

- It takes Courage to be held Accountable without Excuses & Blames!

- It takes courage to take less familiar decisions

- It takes courage to constantly Change oneself for Better!

- It takes courage to give & receive honest Feedback!

- And the courage to shine as bright as you are designed to be and not dimming your shine as per naysayers!

Seasoned leaders develop their skills to take calculated risks thereby reducing the chances of failure. They achieve that by doing a lot of preparation and deliberation and reviewing the risk benefit analysis. Courage and comfort are not friends & Leadership is not a comfortable spot to be in.

Comfort and courage don't go hand in hand as leading and learning; and success is on the other side of comfort, for which courage is essential.

SUCCESS IS ON THE OTHER SIDE OF THE FENCE

Artistic View of Life

How some habits can keep one in the zone of Failure & changing those habits can help cross the fence & jump off to a Successful Life

Failure Traits:	Success Traits:
Indecision	Decisive
Fear	Courage
Self-Doubts	Confidence
Indiscipline	Discipline

To be able to create a life of design and not merely living a default life, one must lead a life of self-control, discipline, hard-work, courage consistently

One is resigned to a default life when:

- When one is indecisive

- When one stays fearful of failure or what people will say attitude and never takes a leap of faith towards his true calling in life.

- When one doubts his own self in terms of confidence, capacity and courage

- When one has habits which are self-destructive whereby he is dreaming about achieving his goals without discipline and self-control

- When one lacks character and integrity

It is only after developing these traits that one develops his best self and is able to break free from living a life of cause and effect and gets in to designing his own life path and leads others too.

Nick: What is failure and why is it on the other side of the fence?

Roy: It is all about a flawed judgement or a faulty habit which when repeated over a long period of time results in failure. On the other hand by making changes in one habit, behavior, self-control, and discipline one can change failure into success. The first step towards crossing the fence is to make a decision and take big consistent action towards.

"He who is not courageous enough to take risks will achieve nothing in Life!"

– Mohammad Ali

(Mohammad Ali was an American professional boxer, activist, and philanthropist. Nicknamed "The

Greatest," he is widely regarded as one of the most significant and celebrated sports figures of the 20th century and as one of the greatest boxers of all time.)

Roy: If a leader is not courageous he simply surrenders or loses his leadership to others, it could be to a colleague, his team, situations, fear, comfort or a bad habit.

Courage builds a capacity to see through rough times. Courage is all about taking decisions and staying accountable for it. Courage is going against the regular decisions and taking a stand for the right thing and ready to face criticism. Courage is about maintaining authenticity as a leader for what you believe in. If we don't stand for what we believe in, we can be easily swayed by what the world wants us to believe in!

Nick: You mean in the absence of courage we become a version of what the world sees us as and not how we see ourselves as? In absence of courage we may stay afraid all our lives and never muster enough courage to step out of our comfort zone thus that is where we stay till the end.

Roy: You just got that right.

Fear is an integral part of everyone's life. Fear is a strong emotion and at times can have significant effect on the judgments/decisions of the leaders. Hence leaders must work upon understanding their emotions.

Nick: *"Emotions can interfere with peoples, ability to achieve their goals and desires*

(Smith, Seger & Mackie 2007)

Nick: Is courage and being fearless one and the same thing?

Roy: Courage is to continue to move towards one's vision inspite of feeling fear. Quoting Nelson Mandela:

"I learned that courage was not the absence of fear, but the triumph over it. The brave man is not he who does not feel afraid, but he who conquers that fear."

– Nelson Mandela

(Nelson Rolihlahla Mandela was a South African anti-apartheid revolutionary, political leader and philanthropist who served as President of South Africa)

Nick: You have just quoted Mohammad Ali the greatest boxer and Nelson Mandela almost back to back!

Roy: Thank you for noticing. Courage is about being fearless as well as about facing challenges with poise and calm.

But let us not make the mistake of misunderstanding courage! Must quote what Winston Churchill said about courage:

"Courage is what it takes to stand up and speak; courage is also what it takes to sit down and listen."

SCALE OF COURAGE HAS TWO PARTS

Face Adversity Bravely	To be Quiet & Listen
Face failure,	To Accept mistakes & take responsibility
Keep moving in face of danger	To Maintain poise under difficult situations

Whereby courage is about standing and speaking up for a cause but at the same time it is equally crucial to shut up and listen and accept if one is wrong or stands to be corrected.

Nick: Thanks Roy for clarifying this misconception, as I always believed that courage was all about speaking and standing up and taking charge of the situation.

Roy: Courage is essential as Leaders have to do the following:

- Drive changes

- Be decisive

- Take risks and face criticism from people

- Holding on to an idea and concept in face of opposition

It takes courage to face your own shortcomings and flaws and overcome them. That is what makes a leader.

Nick: Since courage is at the core of the leadership, does that mean that leadership shines more in trying or difficult situations?

Roy: We all are shaped more by negative experiences than positive ones. Similarly leadership is also forged and gets better often after facing some great negatives experiences.

Leadership Guru Abigail Adams says:

"These are the times in which a genius would wish to live. It is not in the still calm of life, or the repose of a pacific station, that great characters are formed. The habits of a vigorous mind are formed in contending with difficulties. Great necessities call out great virtues. When a mind is raised, and animated by scenes that engage the heart, then those qualities which would otherwise lay dormant, wake into life and form the character of the hero and the statesman."

(Abigail Adams is best known as the wife of former US President John Adams and for her extensive correspondence. She was also the mother of John Quincy Adams who became the sixth president of the United States)

LEADERS ARE SHAPED BY CRISIS & DIFFICULT TIMES!

Nick: Everyone hits a rough patch in life don't they?

Roy: However it's a choice whether we rise up to a situation or we get overwhelmed by the situation and freeze and feel victimized. Success is said to be a lousy teacher however to be in crisis is a great place to learn. Either one breaks down during crisis or ends up adapting & emerge stronger post the crisis. We have a choice to either learn from the most difficult times or take a flight from the situation. The difficult times can be called as "life changing or unexpected traumatic experiences or "hardships." No matter what we call them we can't escape facing them in our lives. This could be a death of a near one, losing a job or business over night, a life threatening illness, close escape from a real bad experience, having faced a war, riots or may be working under an adamant boss. Such an experience leaves us changed as it is during these times we try to ask ourselves questions and introspect to know ourselves better. Sometimes we also end up discovering courage which we never knew we had. It is during these times the best of the leaders see how things fizzle out of their control despite the best of planning. This is the time when we all come face to face with the harsh realities of life no matter how much we are prepared, things are bound to get out of control.

The only thing that we have control on is our response to the situation. This is the time when one is forced to introspect what one stands for and what is one made of, this is also the time to discover ones true authentic self, and uncover all the conditioning of childhood and society

Bennis and Thomas (2002) interviewed more than 40 top leaders in business and in the public sector, and found that all of them went through unplanned, intense, and traumatic experiences that transformed them and developed in them distinct leadership capabilities.

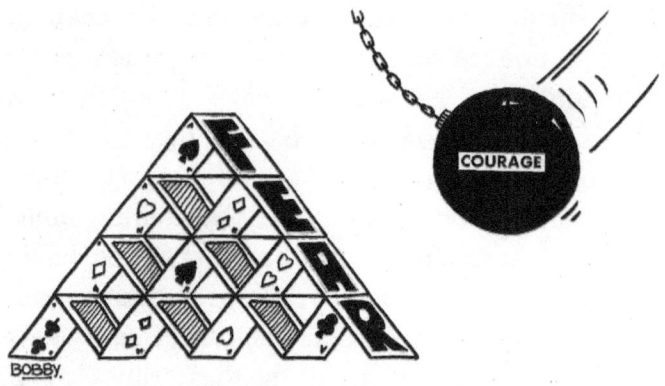

WE MUST SHOW COURAGE IN FACE OF FEAR AND DESTROY FEAR

Obstacles don't have to stop you. If you run into a wall, don't turn around and give up. Figure out how to climb it, go through it, or work around it.

– Michael Jordan

PERSONAL LEADERSHIP

LEADING SELF BEFORE LEADING OTHERS

Your life is a result of choices you have made. If you do not like your life start making better choices.

– Zig Ziglar

"Zig" Ziglar was an American author, salesman, and motivational speaker

"It is not the mountain we conquer but ourselves."

– "Sir Edmund Hillary"

On 29 May 1953, Hillary and Sherpa mountaineer Tenzing Norgay became the first climbers confirmed to have reached the summit of Mount Everest

Nick: What is personal leadership?

Roy: Personal leadership is the ability to focus, develop & utilize our best leadership qualities to guide us to achieve our goals and objectives & not let our life drift in an autopilot mode. It is about making a choice at every step in our life. It is about saying yes to activities that promote us towards vision and saying "NO" to things that stop us from achieving that. It includes choice making, courage, commitment, discipline, hard work, taking action in the direction of our goals. As we build personal leadership we get smarter in productivity, focus, clarity of goals, in short become more focused towards the our goals and the kind of life that we want to live

Building Personal leadership is an essential step towards becoming an effective organizational leader, because people get influenced not by what you say but how you behave. As one improves in leading self, more people get influenced by his consistent, focused & disciplined approach towards goals. Personal leadership development prepares a leader to deal with conflict, change and ambiguous situations more effectively. It is also about managing one's energies effectively in both personal and professional life to be able to live a happy life.

Nick: Does it mean as below?

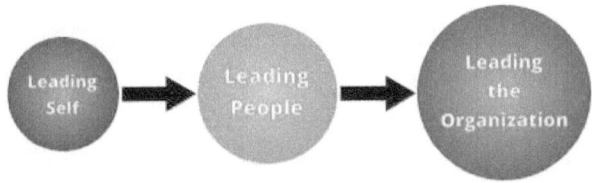

Roy: Yes absolutely. Who is the most important person that you will ever lead?

Nick: I guess myself

Roy: Very True! We are the most important person that we must lead before others. Also leading ourselves is the most challenging work in spite of well knowing our strength, weakness, nature and habits.

Nick: Because change is not an easy business.

Roy: Common mistake that leaders make is that they focus, develop and master the external leadership traits, but often miss inner as well as character development. It is essential for leaders to build character as small flaws left unattended may lead to huge mistakes and organizational problems. Hence it is essential to build strong character which helps in achieving a strong leadership foundation.

Roy: Personal leadership is self-leadership. Personal leadership is the ability to lead one's life towards a particular direction. It's the ability to guide your life rather than letting the circumstances and situations take control of it. Personal leadership is accepting the belief that, I will lead myself and will be completely responsible for the outcomes of all my actions. Personal leadership is leadership of the self. It is the ability to define a role for your life, and to move in that direction with consistency and clarity. Leading yourself means applying the same principles of leadership to your role as a leader of your own life. To become a great leader we must first take charge of ourselves. We need a mission for our lives that gets all of our instincts, habits, passion, and appetites pulling in the same direction.

Nick: Do you mean not to doubt self and not have any conflicting beliefs?

Roy: True! Having conflicting belief is like being pulled equally in two directions!

Nick: What do you mean by that?

Roy: It means more than often we have a split in our mind

We want to do & not want to do something at the same time!

Let me explain this by saying that we all want to stay healthy and fit and for that we must eat healthy, rest and exercise. Most of us want to sincerely go for a walk in the morning and want to wake up early every day but end up sleeping in bed! That actually means that we want to go for a walk and also want to sleep at the same time but we cannot do both.

This has been very well explained by Plato in the allegory of Chariot

Whereby, he compared the soul of a person, to the one driving a chariot, being pulled by two horses. One is white and the other is black and both have wings. By showing the chariot rider with two horses Plato has explained the tripartite nature of the human soul

Plato, in his dialogue *Phaedrus* (sections 246a–254e), uses the Chariot Allegory to explain his concept of the human soul.

1. Dark winged horse: Represents Desires of Body such as Greed, Lust, Pleasure, Money, comfort and warmth

2. White winged horse: Courage, Honour and Nobility of Heart

3. Chariot Driver: Represents – Reason or the rational mind that is trying to control the horses

Abhishek Verma

If the reason is not in control, the horses will run wildly in any direction resulting in being hurt, causing an accident and will deviate from the objective.

It is essential that Charioteer must control the horses effectively, if one is not in control the soul is in chaos!

Hence there is an ongoing inner conflict between: what we want to do and not want to do at the same time.

If the chariot is not in unison with the two horses, then horses end up pulling the chariot into different directions which creates conflict and confusion.

Nick: Is this connected with Integrity?

Roy: Very Right!

"Integrity is doing the right thing even when no one is watching"

– C. S. Lewis

Clive Staples Lewis was a British writer and lay theologian. He held academic positions in English literature at both Oxford University and Cambridge University

Practicing integrity, not out of fear that someone will find about our acts but driven out of self-commitment.

"Earn your leadership every day."

– Michael Jordan – is the greatest basketball player of all time

Nick: How does Personal Leadership transform one's life?

Roy: It is all about achieving clarity towards one's aims and goals and then channelizing one's enterprise towards the same. It is rejecting a default life which comes our way anyhow but it is about transforming one's life with confidence, clarity and enterprise. It is not about working aiming merely to survive but it is about aiming to succeed and be our true self.

Personal Leadership is about discovering our best potential rather than living in oblivion. It is about encouraging self for doing and excelling in our visions and dreams!

It is about trusting and moving ahead confidently to face challenges. Building Personal Leadership is crucial to building organizational leadership. Personal leadership is about investing in one's learning, skills and potential. Developing self contributes in all areas of life including professional as well as personal. It will make one work smarter, more productive and efficient.

Nick: It will also lead to more clarity towards ones goals, objectives, strategies and how to better achieve them.

Personal leadership is a stepping stone towards effective Life leadership.

Roy: It helps leaders to get a better insight of themselves and their behavior.

They develop intense commitment and discipline which helps them in all their endeavors. This behavior leads to building character and results in achieving trust and authenticity with teams.

- It sharpens the skills of the leaders to spearhead

- It also ensures that leadership does not fail or becomes ineffective because of lacking in personal traits.

- Personal Leadership also fiercely aims at leaders' energy as it is crucial for the leader to work tirelessly emotionally and physically.

- One discovers own blind spots, areas where one needs to work upon

- Helps leaders introspect and reflect on their own behavior which makes them better

- By knowing self, leaders are able to exercise better control on self, leading to inspiring behavior and improved performance of self as well as the team.

Nick: Personal Leadership is a challenge, as it is easy to preach but challenging to rein your horses and stay focused on your goals in this world which is so full of distractions.

"If you want to be the best you have to do things that other people are not willing to do."

– Anonymous

LEADERS MUST HAVE CLARITY OF VISION

If one does not know which port one is sailing, no wind is favourable!

– Lucius Annaeus Seneca

Seneca, was a Roman Stoic philosopher, statesman, dramatist, and—in one work—satirist of the Silver Age of Latin literature

Roy: Clarity of vision is the first step towards achieving excellence & clarity of vision is the first step towards achieving a vision

We must ask ourselves:

- Who do we serve?

- Where are we heading?

- Why does our work matter?

- What are we doing?

- What are the most important things that we should be doing?

- What value we provide?

- What are our core strengths?

- How are performing (measuring our performance)?

- What values & qualities are essential to our work?

- How can I contribute more?

- How can we leverage our team's strengths?

- How can we get better and contribute more? These are some of the questions that drive clarity in vision.

Nick: How do leaders achieve clarity which they communicate simply?

Roy: They reflect, think & introspect. This is something most of the people miss to do in their day to day activity and excuse simply by telling themselves that they are too busy and have no time.

Also leaders look upto the ideals and how they have done and would have behaved in the circumstances and learn from them and they practice and keep fine tuning their art of leadership. Also vision must be well communicated to the entire team and care to be taken that it is understood in the spirit it is meant to be

NOTHING MOVES WITHOUT LABOUR LEADERS WORK HARD!

Dreams are free. Goals have a cost. While you can day dream for free, goals don't come without a price, Time, Effort, Sacrifice, and Sweat. How will you pay for your goals?

– Usain Bolt

Owing to his achievements and dominance in sprint competition, he is widely considered to be the greatest sprinter of all time

Do what is easy and your life would be hard, do what is hard and your life would be easy!

– Les Brown

Leslie Calvin "Les" Brown is an American motivational speaker, author, former radio DJ, and former television host

Nick: I have often heard that leaders are hard-working, disciplined and display a lot of self-control! Is that true

Roy: The answer to that lies in another question!

Are you working to survive? Or working to succeed and to make your dream come true?

Nick: To make our dreams come true!!

Roy: Then you are definitely going to need a big dose of hard work, discipline and self-control.

Roy: Hard work vs. Work

Work is what you do just to survive and hard work is what you do to succeed.

WORK MEANT FOR MERE SURVIVAL	HARDWORK & INTELLIGENT WORK ENSURES SUCCESS

Roy: Hope the above explains the concept of hard-work!

Nick: What is intelligent work?

Roy: It is about Pareto's Principle or the rule of 80/20

(Management consultant Joseph M. Juran suggested the principle and named it after Italian economist Vilfredo Pareto, who noted the 80/20 connection while at the University of Lausanne in 1896, as published in his first work, Coursd' économie politique)

In short it is about 20% our result come from 80% efforts

And 80% of our results come from 20% of our effort

Nick: How is that achieved?

Roy: That is achieved by

Investing 80% of our efforts on the Vital Few aspects of the business

(Vital few aspects are the key areas which affect the results)

It means 80% of the results are outcome of 20% of causes.

Thereby by concentrating and focusing on 20% of the causes one can change 80% of the results.

Nick: So in a way it's an intelligent approach towards committing time and resources, as all causes do not have equal impact on the result.

Can you help me with some application examples?

Roy: for example 80% of Smart phone owners only use 20% of its features

Or 80% of business comes from 20% of customers

80% of the world's wealth is owned by 20% of the people of the world.

Nick: Got that well!

Pareto's principle

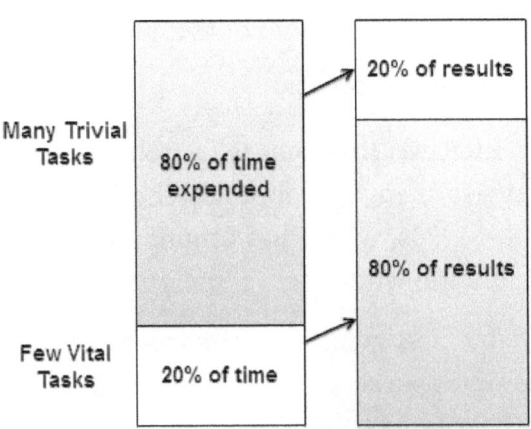

Oxford defines hard work as, "a great deal of effort or endurance."

Merriam-Webster defines hardworking as, "industrious and diligent."

Nick: But what about the saying an overnight success?

Roy: Have you heard of the following people:

– Lionel Messi – Steve Jobs – Richard Branson

Nick: Of course I know!

Lionel Messi:

Lionel Andrés Messi Cuccittini is an Argentine professional footballer

Steve Jobs:

Steven Paul Jobs-Chairman, Chief Executive Officer, and Co-Founder of Apple Inc)

Richard Branson:

Sir Richard Branson is a self-made British business man who founded the Virgin Group in the 1970s, which has around 400 companies around the world)

Roy: Let us see what they have to say about overnight success?

Lionel Messi: "*It took me 17 years and 114 days to become an overnight success*"

Steve Jobs: "*If you really look closely, most of the overnight success stories took a long time*"

Richard Branson: "*There are no quick wins in Business – It takes years to become an overnight success!*"

It is not about talent, I recall Stephen King the famous author calling talent cheaper than table salt. The world is full of talented people who never excelled or succeeded.

Nick: I am able to connect the dots. So you mean there is no such thing as over-night success! It only seems so to us as we have not seen the discipline, struggle, preparation & frustration part of the winners.

Roy: See we only get to see the success of the legendary performers, but do not realize how many years they have been practicing and fine tuning there art or skill. It is in a way like an ice berg

Nick: Iceberg (is a floating mass of freshwater ice, which is 80–90% submerged in water and only 10% of its tip is visible)

You mean to say that we get to see only 10% of the success that the leaders achieve as they succeed but fail to see the sweat, slogging, hard work, and struggle they have gone through. We don't see the efforts and sleepless nights they have spent to be where they are today and hence we contemplate it to be an overnight success.

VISIBLE SUCCESS IS LIKE AN ICE-BERG

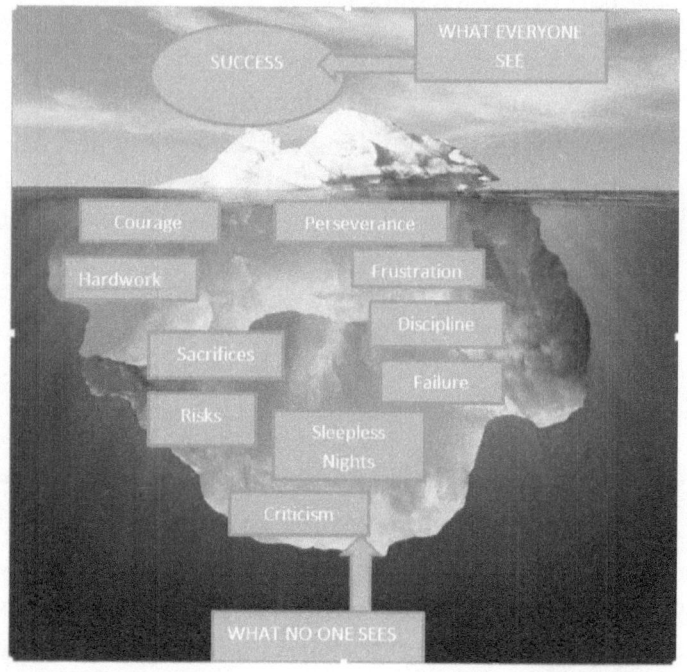

Roy: Leadership is lot of hard work and to do that one must have energy. Hence leaders must manage their energy as they are the role models. They must first look after their health and fitness as that sets the tone too in the organization. Looking after health and fitness includes rest, diet, mental and spiritual fitness as well.

Nick: Is health and fitness not one and the same thing?

Roy: Health is about having a body which is free from disease and fitness is about being able to perform certain physical activities like stretching, flexibility, stamina, strength, agility & power.

Roy: Absolutely. The journey is practice, practice and practice a little more even if you don't like it.... To become a professional

Practice can be utterly boring and frustrating.

Practicing tasks endlessly can be very daunting

Practicing without results for a considerable period of time is discouraging

Practicing is facing repeated failure and never giving up

PRACTICE IS THE BUILDING BLOCK OF SUCCESS

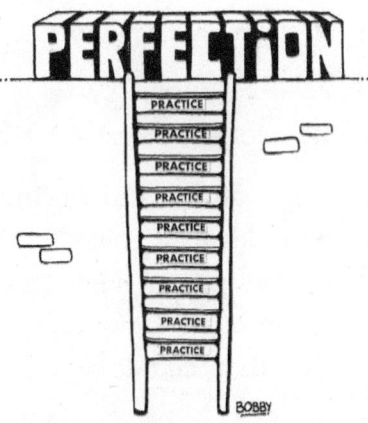

LADDER OF SUCCESS – EXCELLENCE – PERFECTION

That is what is finally recognized and rewarded because most people would give it up!

"We are what we repeatedly do, excellence then is not an act, but a habit."

– Aristotle

Nick: I find practicing extremely boring, yet I keep it going! Can you help me a little more to understand the value of practice?

Roy: There is no short cut to practice; hence it must become a habit like brushing teeth or having a shower! Doing same thing over and over again is for sure boring yet it is the most critical element in developing expertise or excellence.

   I recall Outliers, Malcolm Gladwell suggests that it requires 10000 hours of practice to become an expert.

Nick: What is the relevance of practice in leadership?

Roy: Practicing is painful and boring that is the reason some leaders resist it. They believe once they have got an idea or concept, they know well enough how to apply and use it. However that could be a misconception as learning new technology or concepts is painful as it takes time, repeated trials, can be frustrating and numerous corrections which makes leaders shirk away from that and they may be tempted going back to their old ways of doing things. I have often observed that certain orthodox leadership positions refrain from doing much effort in the digital media as that requires them to learn the subject before they indulge in that professionally. To keep going and continuous improvement must be fueled with passion as "Passion" is that fuel that keeps hard work going.

As mentioned in one of the speech by Steve Job that

"People say you have to have a lot of passion for what you're doing and it's absolutely true the reason being because it's so hard, and if you don't, any rational person would give up"

LEADERS MUST BE SKILLED

Roy: Being only competent does not qualify one to be a leader but not being competent may disqualify one's ability to lead. Leaders may not be essentially qualified to do everything in an organization but they must know what all is to be done, how to get that done and anticipate any roadblocks in achieving the purpose. All this understanding requires competency.

Level of Competencies:

Leaders must delegate and to delegate they must know their own as well as the competencies of their team members.

There are four levels of competencies:

1. **Unconscious Incompetence**: It is an individual who is not skilled and is not even aware of the fact that he is unskilled. This is a sure recipe for disaster as he does not even work to upgrade his skills, as he feels otherwise.

2. **Conscious Incompetence**: It is an individual who is not skilled but is aware of the fact that he needs to learn to be skilled. Since he is aware of his weakness and areas of development and is being honest about it, there is good scope that he will be able to develop the skill with sincere efforts.

3. **Conscious Competence**: It is an individual who is skilled and is aware of his skills as well. This level of team members can be relied upon for delegation by the leader and they mostly deliver as per the expectations.

This level can be achieved by unconscious incompetent level team members & conscious incompetent level of team members by continuous and sincere efforts and practice.

4. **Unconscious Competence**: It is that level of people who are masters of their craft and skills, those who are champions in there league. Names like Roger Federer (Tennis), Virat Kohli (Cricket), Michael Jordan (Basketball) or Tiger Woods (Golf) to name a few.

Nick: At unconscious expert level player do not have to think before playing a shot, it just happens. They have practiced the craft at such a high level that things smoothly happen on its own, making others believe that it is simple and they can also do it. But it only seems so because the masters execute it with so much ease and brilliance.

Nick: Often leaders are appointed on basis of their competency? Is that the best assessment?

Roy: Most of the business schools and education institutes focus on developing skills and competencies, but they miss out on teaching some of the skills which truly matter. Similarly most of the companies hire people for leadership positions based on their skill and competency. They should also be assessing the character and moral values of the leaders as that would have a lasting impact on the organizational culture for years to come.

What I mean to say is that often organizations over emphasize on the skill and competency of the leader and under estimate the character and moral value requirements in the leadership role while hiring. Though competency and skill is an essential requirement to lead but not having that can create numerous errors in judgement leading any organization to decline.

Nick: I completely agree with this! For example the education system teaches and trains more on speaking skills but does not educate to be patient listener which is so crucial in communication.

Roy: There is a great opportunity to educate and coach leadership applicable at both personal and professional level.

Nick: It is also said by Socrates

"One who clearly knows best what ought to be done, will most easily gain the obedience of the others."

FOR BIGGER RESULTS PRACTICE:
SELF CONTROL & DISCIPLINE

"Anybody can become angry — that is easy, but to be angry with the right person and to the right degree and at the right time and for the right purpose, and in the right way — that is not within everybody's power and is not easy."

Socrates was a classical Greek philosopher credited as one of the founders of Western philosophy, and as being the first moral philosopher of the Western ethical tradition of thought.

Roy: Self-control is the quality or ability to control oneself from doing things which may not be in the best interest of one self. Often we knowingly keep doing things which may not be in our best of interest just because we have been doing them as a habit or as per our conditioning.

Nick: Does self-discipline means leaders should control their anger and stay calm always?

Roy: The possession of self-discipline enables one to choose, and persevere in actions thoughts and behavior, which lead to improvement and success. It also gives one the power and inner strength to overcome addictions, anger, procrastination and laziness to follow through the initiatives undertaken.

Leaders have to fit in the shoes of expectations, not only of those who follow them but of their own as well. In fact leaders have almost challenging expectations from themselves. They have firm belief that they can achieve what they have set their eyes on in spite of no one trusting them. Self-discipline means doing what needs to be done even if we don't feel like it.

Some of us wait for motivation to strike us to start doing things that are required to be done and don't do that till we feel motivated. Self-Discipline is doing things that need to be done even if we feel de motivated.

Nick: Can you tell me why do we avoid getting self-disciplined?

Roy: The key reason why most of the people don't practice self-discipline is because they are tuned for instant results.

Just like hard work, disciplining personal and professional life is not easy. It takes a lot of effort. But this is the choice that will define what we achieve in life. With little self-discipline, we end up achieving lesser and with more discipline we tend to achieve more success! So the result of discipline is success and lack of discipline is a lot of pain and regret.

Nick: What are the reasons why people avoid being self –disciplined?

Roy: One of the key reasons is most of the people are accustomed to instant results and gratification for their efforts!

Most of us come with a belief that if we have put in some effort its results must be visible, which is the hope of instant results/gratification.

THE CONCEPT OF DELAYED GRATIFICATION SECRET TO SUCCESS

Roy: Have you heard of the marshmallow test?

Nick: Yes I have in my research!

The Stanford marshmallow experiment was a series of studies on delayed gratification in the late 1960s and early 1970s led by psychologist Walter Mischel, then a professor at Stanford University.

The test was conducted on kids whereby they were taken inside a room and were given two options:

Take one marshmallow immediately and leave or

wait for few hours and take two or more marshmallows.

The study findings were those children who persevered and waited longer for additional marshmallow did well in life too and were more successful than the kids who yielded to instant gratification and ended up taking one marshmallow immediately and left.

Roy: The character aspect of persevering for delayed gratification is one of the key characteristics of leaders. This is the same quality which builds great athletes, sport legends and even musicians and of course business leaders as well. I know being a musician & sports lover this resonates well with you.

Nick: You got me.

Roy: Often people work on a dream for a while and when they see no tangible results, they quit. For example, if we start going to a fitness center tomorrow onwards and check our muscles in a couple of days! Will they show any difference?

Nick: No!

Roy: And if you continue to exercise regularly for few months would your physical appearance change?

Nick: Yes it will! But what is the point?

Roy: It is only be after a considerable period of time that we are able to see the noticeable difference in our body. However, most of the people who don't see any tangible results in their short term efforts, quit. On the other hand leaders know that it takes a lot of patience before tangible difference is visible to the world. There are numerous examples from which one can learn the same phenomenon. For example:

Chinese Bamboo Plantation is a classic example to learn. It is always said if you are impatient never plant a Chinese bamboo seed.

Nick: Why is that?

Roy: It is probably the best example of patience learning from nature:

Bamboo seed when planted like any other seed requires sunlight, water & good soil

1st Year: After one year of taking care, no growth is visible.

2nd Year: After two years if taken care again, no growth is visible.

3rd Year & 4th Year: After 3rd & 4th year of taking care again, no growth is visible.

5th Year: But in the 5th year suddenly it shoots up to 80 feet in just 6–7 weeks.

This means that till the initial 4 years no tangible growth is visible and it seems that the seed will not sprout at all and got lost but in reality the seed was gaining ground and growing roots to grow taller when its time comes.

Nick: I got what it means.

Similarly, during the initial efforts when results are not visible it seems that efforts have failed and majority of the people quit believing that they have failed. However, it is just a part of the process to achieve success.

Nick: That was such a beautiful analogy to explain the importance & concept of delayed gratification in leadership.

Roy: Thank you for appreciating.

The world is full of stories of path breaking leaders who have lived the secret of delayed gratification. They understand that just because results are not visible does not mean they are not on a growth path.

They also do not seek external recognition as a sole means for their success.

As the famous quote from Thomas Edison, when someone asked him that why he failed often while inventing the light bulb?

Edison's reply was:

"I haven't failed! I just found 10000 ways that won't work"

---

100 years ago Henry Longfellow said beautifully in a poem:

"The heights by great men reached and kept

Were not attained by sudden flight,

But they, while their companions slept,

Toiled ever upward through the night."

Nick: But isn't it easier said than done! We must discuss what takes them through their difficult or struggling times?

Roy: Leaders know very well that failure is a part of leadership similar to as when a business is started profit and loss are an integral part of it. They also accept failure as part of their role and journey.

Roy: Some of the reasons most of the people don't succeed or fail to lead in their personal lives?

- Lack of Self Esteem!

- Poor Health and Energy!

- Over Planning & No Action!

- Lack of Purpose & Direction!

- Procrastination Habits!

- Because they quit at the slightest obstacle

- Fear of Failure!

- Lack of Self Control & Discipline!

- Fearing what People Will Say about them!

- They have been conditioned to believe that they are mediocre people and will always live a mediocre life!

Nick: In fact I have made a charter of excuses on why we don't do things which we should be doing?

CHARTER OF "EXCUSES"

- I don't have enough time

- I am too old for this

- I am too young for this

- Life is not fair

- Why this happens to me always

- My circumstances don't allow me

- I don't have enough resources

- I am not ready for this yet

- I have tried this before & failed

- This is simply impossible

- My family never supports me

In fact often people start believing that their version of themselves is what the world thinks them to be and not what they truly are. Not staying authentic to one's true self can be self-destructive! One needs self-discipline to change and become what one wants to be.

We must know the price that is paid by not being self-disciplined?

Nick: What is that price?

Roy: A Life full of regret. Life is a continuous battle between comfort and going courageously for our dreams and purpose. It is easy to slip into a comfort and life of ease and not disciplining ourselves. This easily leads many towards a life which is aimless and purposeless. Life of ease is all about small achievements, status quo, wavering decisions & unfinished dreamy projects.

Little discipline little achievements, more the discipline more the achievements. It easy to live an unorganized and undisciplined life, which is living by default, leading to failure and regret!

Nick: And selected few are willing to pay that price and live a fulfilling life and those who choose an easy undisciplined way live a mediocre life and often end up with the guilt of not having tried to be what they could have!

Nick: Easier said than done, in today's life there is so much to do and so little time.

Roy: Excuses are many for non-starters to never initiate a dream project that they always wanted to. Why don't you create a charter of no excuses?

CHARTER OF "NO EXCUSES"

Although the world is full of suffering,
it is also full of the overcoming of it.

– Hellen Keller-

Have a clear vision about life & goals

- **Don't major in minor issues of life
- Decide, commit and take big action towards their vision
- Keep learning continuously & investing in themselves and re-invent
- Take full responsibility of actions without blaming others
- Refuse to quit in the face of set back and failures
- Know failure is a process to achieve success
- Give 100% effort to the committed vision
- See opportunities where excusers see pain & hard-work

**Majoring in Minors: Tendency to focus on minor things in life and committing more time to them & missing to commit time & energy to major and important things in life.

Roy: We often have to ask ourselves the following questions:

What are we busy doing?

And are we busy majoring in minors?

Which means are we spending our day on issues which don't matter in the bigger picture of our objective or we are busy doing the most important activities which push us towards our goals

Roy: We have two choices about how we run our day

Jim Rohn answers that too for us.

"Either the day runs you or you run the day!!"

– Jim Rohn

Roy: Do you want to live a Life of Design or a Life of Default?

Nick: I would request for more insight into this concept?

LIFE OF DEFAULT

Living life in an autopilot mode

Living without a purpose & goal

Surrendering the power of making a choice to circumstances

No well-defined plan to achieve goals

Not taking any big action towards goals

No consistency in efforts

Sleepwalking through life aimlessly

Living without an objective & trying to fit into the herd

Missing to seize the opportunities

Continued feeling of being stuck & victimized

Often full of blaming others

LIFE OF DESIGN

Taking complete charge of one's life

Having clarity of purpose, direction & goals

Making a choice to create a life what one wants to.

Asserting ones intentions to achieve goals

Willingness to plan & take action towards one's goals

Making consistent efforts & committing 100% to one's dreams & goals

It is about facing obstacles and hardships with courage & grit

Taking responsibility for consequences of one's actions

Nick: How can one move from, living a life of default to living a life of design?

Roy: To answer that simply, one should have clarity of purpose, belief and take a leap of faith!

Leap of faith may be explained as believing in results or outcomes even in the absence of any credible or strong evidence. This happens often in organizations as well as in personal lives, that in spite of all the efforts and information available one is unable to reach a decisive conclusion

Nick: Is it some kind of a gut feel, inner voice or an expertise to predict future results even in the absence of any concrete supporting information

Roy: You got that right

Nick: Tell me more about life of design and life of default?

Roy: Life of default is living a life which simply comes our way; it is living life on an auto pilot mode

Nick: Which means the autopilot is in charge, not you!

Roy: It is about not taking charge of one's life

Nick: Is it like sleep walking through our lives

Roy: True, just going through life mindlessly and without knowing that the everyday behavior or choices are moving us away or closer to what we want in our lives

LIVING A LIFE OF DESIGN

Roy: Is living a life of design all about asserting your intentions and taking charge. It is about questioning the status quo and also taking action with courage to change it. It is to move towards what one wants, aspires to be, achieve or serve

It is about setting clear well defined goals and committing all efforts and resources to achieve them

Nick: I am keen to know how this work?

How do I know if I am living life on autopilot mode by default?

Roy: Let me ask you some questions about defining Sense of Purpose?

- Do you have a well-defined purpose or goal?

- Do you take big actions towards your goals consistently?

Nick: You mean having a plan of action towards our goals!

Roy: Yes! The road to design life & to achieve our purpose is hard, and if we lack purpose and passion we may give it up when we face obstacles.

Do you get up excited every morning to aggressively pursue your goals and objectives?

I am sure Ikigai knowledge would be useful for you

Nick: What is ikigai

Nick: Help me understand how does one create that compelling vision or purpose of life? Do you mean:

"Where your talents and the world's needs meet is where you will find your vocation."

– Aristotle

Roy: Japanese in Okinawa region know something which the world should know?

Ikigai! Is all about what your purpose of being is?

Roy: Ikigai is the answer to the question which you wanted to ask earlier?

Nick: I was about to ask, that most of the people don't know what they want or aspire or look forward to in their lives?

Ikigai is a Japanese concept that simply means,

"The reason to get out of the bed every morning"

It's a combination of two words

1. Iki: Life or living

2. Gai: Values

"Our intuition and curiosity are very powerful internal compasses to help us connect with our ikigai,"

'iki' which translates to 'life,' and 'gai' which is used to describe value or worth, ikigai means finding joy in life through purpose.

– Hector Garcia and Francesc Miralles

Roy: The below IKIGAI model is amazing.

The concept is best illustrated by the overlapping circles and the four circles represent:

1. What you love?

2. What you are good at?

3. What the world needs?

4. What you are/could be paid for?

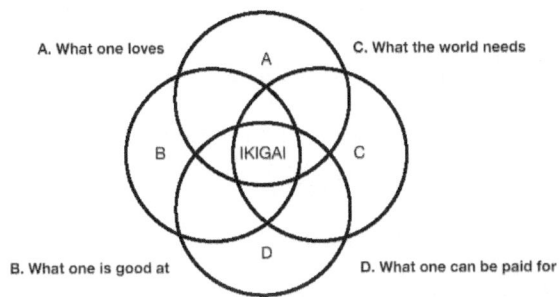

Nick: Philosopher and civil rights leader Howard W Thurman said,

---

"Ask what makes you come alive and go do it." ... "Don't ask what the world needs. Ask what makes you come alive, and go do it. Because what the world needs are the people who have come alive."

Roy: In their book Ikigai The Japanese Secret to a Long and Happy Life, Hector Garcia and Francesc Miralles have mentioned ten rules to find one's ikigai:

1. Stay active and don't retire

2. Leave urgency behind and adopt a slower pace of life

3. Only eat until you are 80 per cent full

4. Surround yourself with good friends

5. Get in shape through daily, gentle exercise

6. Smile and acknowledge people around you

7. Reconnect with nature

8. Give thanks to anything that brightens our day and makes us feel alive

9. Live in the moment

10. Follow your ikigai

Nick: Does this mean that if we are able to find joy in what we do and if one excels in it that is when we have found our ikigai?

Roy: Smiles!!

Leadership must establish a common purpose to achieve within a sense of timeline. The key task is to share a concrete & clear vision with the team.

Along with creating synergized team towards the goals/vision through communication of the goals:

- Transform

- Create more leaders

- Achieve the vision

- Overcome obstacles

- Providing direction in the new uncharted path ever before

- Break the status quo by innovating

They create accountability for self and hence inspire others also to be self-accountable for the progress and not indulge in blame game. They aim at achieving a culture based on sense of collaboration and not competing against each other. Create an environment of trust and humility

However for living and achieving a life that one wants, there is no alternative to discipline.

Nick: I understand that now, staying focused and true to one's vision is possible with self-discipline in leadership.

Roy: Some of the results of Self Discipline in leadership are:

- Strengthens inner character and strength
- Improves consistency, which leads to more chances to succeed
- Improves Focus
- Increase in overall standards
- Increase in confidence as You Focus on priorities
- Improved productivity.
- Better day and time management.
- On way to success
- More self-reliance and control of one's life
- Lesser guilt and becoming more of your true self

Roy: If we do not impose discipline in our life, we unknowingly invite a situation where someone else will force us to get disciplined. We should be constantly watchful of our life situation before it goes out of hand. For example often doctors force discipline in the life of their patients by either subjecting them to medication or surgery which could have been prevented if they took good care of their body by exercising, controlling their diet and living a healthy lifestyle. Lot many patients are hooked to a restricted change in their life style as they have gone too far in abusing their body, mind or soul.

Nick: So in a way self-discipline and self-control actually give us long term freedom to live the way we want to live. It gives freedom from living up to expectations of others and moves towards living to self-expectations. It beats down lethargy and procrastination.

So Self-discipline actually provides more freedom

Roy: You see nothing comes for free; we must pay the price of self-discipline to achieve complete freedom. Discipline has its own rewards and lack of it leads to self-pity and regret.

Self-discipline is self-empowering, it boosts ones confidence in self and gives freedom from doubt and fears. It gives wings to the dreams & goals and fuels our inner. The first step to self-discipline is to control what we think and speak! The mind tends to believe what we believe! What-ever we think grows, if we fuel our thoughts with self-doubt it grows, if we fuel our thoughts with self-belief, faith in our abilities to accomplish, they grow. More discipline is more freedom.

Nick: Let me recite here ages old" The two wolf story, which we must have heard before but it's a great reminder to all of us to redirect our course of navigation in life

Abhishek Verma

Story of the Two-Wolf Fight Going With-in Us Between – The Good Wolf Vs Evil Wolf

An old Cherokee is teaching his grandson lessons about life! He says listen son:

Inside each of us there are two wolves, an evil wolf and a good wolf and they are constantly engaged in a terrible fight!

The evil wolf represents: anger, jealousy, resentment, hatred, inferiority, guilt, ego, greed, arrogance and false pride

The good wolf represents: hope, faith, peace, love, serenity, empathy, compassion, generosity and kindness

The grandson is patiently listening and asks: In this fight which wolf wins?

The Old Cherokee answers: "The one you feed"

Nick: Leadership is all about the winning of the Good wolf and defeating the evil wolf and if the evil wolf is winning we get negative or pseudo leaders.

LEADERSHIP IS BY CHOICE

"I am not a product of my circumstances. I am a product of my decisions."

– Dr. Stephen R. Covey

(Stephen Richards Covey was an American educator, author, businessman, and keynote speaker. His most popular book is The 7 Habits of Highly Effective People)

Roy: Choice is a freedom and Leadership in itself is a choice!

Different choices that leaders make are following:

- Leaders choose a purpose,

- They choose courage to follow their purpose

- They choose a skill

- They choose courage over fear

- They choose action over comfort

- They choose to commit themselves

- They choose perseverance to change the status quo and commit relentlessly to achieve their targets.

- They choose to believe themselves over doubting themselves

- They choose to develop themselves,

- They choose to re-invent themselves,

- They choose to take responsibility & accountability

- They choose to engage with their teams and lead them to success

- They choose to care about their teams

- They choose to develop & invest in their team!

- They choose that they have a choice and just merely a victim of circumstances

They are aware that they have a choice in all situations and hence don't feel victimized. They are there to make a difference and not follow the herd.

Leadership is not by chance but it is by making choices in our lives.

Roy: An individual's behavior and personality is a result of

- Upbringing

- Conditioning

- Childhood experiences

- Parents treatments

- Friends

- Society around

- Education & Schooling

We tend to believe that the image formed out of those experiences and conditions is what we are, how we live and conduct our entire life in a cocoon.

Nick: I get that, there is also a great song on that by Pink Floyd:

"Another brick in the wall" song is all about living in an autopilot mode just trying to fit in the system and not trying to make choices and make a difference.

But can we change and become what we always wanted to be?

Roy: Yes what we were always designed to be, you mean!

But often we stop that discovery, by creating our own barriers.

Nick: You mean often we are the ones stopping ourselves from becoming our best selves!

Roy: True! We all have different conditioning and most of us remain caged and end up sleep walking through life which is an expected trend that we have been subjected to live by. Often we stay caged in our own image which is actually not our true self. It is an image we are living against rather than living or expressing our true self. We somehow get imprisoned to our personality and don't change.

Nick: However few people are able to discover their true potential and re-invent themselves

Roy: By introspection and by using the power of choice, their life changes to a life of design from an auto pilot mode living. As a result of that they discover their true self.

Change happens when we seize the power of knowing that we have the power to choose a response and realizing that there are unlimited choices. But often we get clouded by our conditioning, fear and emotions and end up taking decisions based on our conditioning.

To change our course of life and results we cannot make the most common mistake of repeating the same inputs and expecting different results. We must exercise the untapped power of choices that we have between what happens and how we react to that. We need to know that we are free to make choices and that freedom of making choices is leadership.

We can choose how we feel

We can choose our emotions

We can choose our beliefs

We can choose our values

We can choose how to react to failure

We can choose how to react to fear

We can choose to bounce back or stay down after a set back

We can choose to believe that we can win or not?

Roy: A person, who is reactive, is powerless and is unaware, that he has choices and believes that he has no control over the situation or results.

On the other hand people who are proactive, know that they have the power to choose, and choose their response accordingly.

Unknowing most of people's actions are a result of cause and effect and not out of willful choices. Most of us live a life of default which is our conditioning, and leaders by reflecting and using the power to choose live a life of design.

Nick: That sounds so tragic for some and magical for the others. And most of the time, we are under the impression that we have created our whole life out of free will!

Roy: To escape a prison one needs to know that he is in a prison, if he does not even know that, how can he ever break out of that prison, this is one of the biggest tragedy.

Roy: Unless we exercise the power of choice and break away from the cause and effect life.

Roy: That is why the quote that says:

"The best way to keep a prisoner from escaping is to make sure he never knows he's in prison."

– Fyodor Dostoyevsky

(Was a Russian novelist, short story writer, essayist, journalist and philosopher)

That is the reason that sometimes our achievements feel shallow as they don't match with who we truly are and wanted to be!

Nick: Why don't we exercise our power of choice?

Roy: We all in our hearts know what we want to be and what we truly are but the problem is we refuse to listen to that inner voice and the naysayers around us discourage us to take a path which is meant for us. So we simply follow the loud voices around us and end up pursuing what everyone is doing or telling us to comply with. We tend to borrow the same fears & somewhat similar values of the people around us. Also we are afraid to follow or believe what our inner voice say, as it may lead us to a lesser known path and hence we are afraid to leave our comfort zone and predictable state of life and end up following the herd mentality

Nick: What is herd mentality?

Roy: It's the tendency of people to behave as per the group that they are in! It's a natural desire to behave as per the crowd and become a part of it.

This leads to poor decision making, as a result of that one starts behaving as per the crowd behavior rather than depending on one's own intellect.

(Herd Mentality is the mentality, behaviour or thinking of a herd, group or a pack of peole which is completely influenced by the peers they are sorrounded by. The behaviour is not based on rationality)

Don't Go for the Majority,
Follow the Right Way!

Roy: Herd mentality driven people are happy being in the status quo! Leaders shake that status of comfort zone and share a higher vision and purpose leading everyone to outperform their own expectations. Leaders provide a collective and shared vision and communicate and convince the teams to create joint effort to achieve vision

Nick: Steve Jobs has defined that well for us to learn from

Don't be trapped by dogma—which is living with the results of other people's thinking. Don't let the noise of other's opinions drown out your own inner voice. And most important, have the courage to follow your heart and intuition. They somehow already know what you truly want to become. Everything else is secondary."

– Steve Jobs

PURPOSE OF LEADERSHIP IS TO MAKE MORE LEADERS

Abhishek Verma

Artistic view of a Lion carrying Sheep's inside

A Lion Leader can inspire Sheep's to be Courageous

"I am not afraid of an army of lions led by a sheep; I am afraid of an army of sheep led by a lion."

– Alexander the Great

Nick: I cannot hold the story of a lion cub which lived like a sheep!

Once there was a lion, which grew up amongst a flock of sheep, not knowing that he was a lion. He ate grass and behaved like the other sheep. One day while wandering in the forest a Lion jumped in front of the sheep flock, the entire flock started running around trying to save themselves from the lion. The Lion was surprised to see lion amongst the group of the sheep, so he got hold of that lion. This Lion starting behaving like a sheep and was scared that the lion will eat him up. The other lion took him to a river and showed him who he was. The lion from the herd of sheep saw his reflection in the river and looked at the other lion. And he was never a sheep again and immediately discovered that he was a lion.

Nick: How tragic it is that we often are lions and have surrendered to living a life of a sheep!

Roy: Leaders are those lions who not only know that they are lions but also inspire others to be lions. They not only break away from the herd mentality themselves but also guide others to tap into their hidden potential. They even have the capability to make sheep's believe that they are lions and inspire them to behave like one.

Roy: Courage is one of the defining qualities of leadership!

Nick: What are some of the qualities of courageous leaders?

Roy: They take bold decisions even when they face criticism or even if it makes them less popular or disliked! They create a new path for themselves and the team. They hold people and themselves accountable. They handle issues head on and don't beat around the bush. They lead from the front and take responsibility for the consequences.

Nick: I wonder how leaders are able to turn a bunch of fearful sheep into courageous, lion like behavior. It is unbelievable that leaders can have this level of influence.

Roy: Sheep here refers to those who are addicted to comfort and are resistant to change. Sheep obediently follow the shepherd who gives them a feeling of security. It takes a lion like behavior to explain it to them that the real purpose is not to follow the master (in this case a shepherd) but to pursue mastery or excellence. He challenges the intellect of the sheep. The sheep have lived long under fear and have never faced change. The lion shows them a behavior which is not afraid to change or moving in unknown territories, sheep have never been to before, they start getting influenced. When a leader behaves out of courage, sheep begin to ask questions and ponder if being courageous is the way to go

Nick: Some of the naturally courageous sheep immediately join the lions and some later as the certain culture of this infectious courage takes over.

Comfort is addictive that is why this process is not at over-night process and takes time. So it is upto the courageous leader to keep helping, coaching, encouraging, communicating & empowering.

Nick: It is like when a sheep falls, they support them stand again and slowly the sheep start to show courageous behavior, and start to question the status quo. That is how sheep begun to become leaders.

Roy: It is the same way that organizational courage and empowerment is achieved by leaders by continuously encouraging teams to do better and supporting them. Often company's culture is based on fear and not courage! The fear based organizations have a toxic environment where people hold their ideas and opinions since they fear being ridiculed and snubbed. However courage based organization encourages open door discussion, respects opinions and suggestions of everyone for the betterment of the shared vision

Nick: The true purpose of leadership is to create more leader

Roy: Let me share an effective model that assists in learning about self, others and helps in building trust.

Johari Window Model (19550) was developed by Joseph Luft and Harrington Ingham. It was developed to understand ourselves and our relationships with others. The model is based on two key principles:

1. Listening openly to feedback helps learn more about self and guides further areas of development

2. Communication & sharing information about self builds trust with people

It has four quadrants of this model is drawn below

There are four areas in

• Open Space: Known to you – Known to others. ...

• Blind Spot: Unknown to yourself – Known to others. ...

- Hidden Area: Known to yourself – Unknown to others. ...

- Unknown Area: Unknown to yourself – Unknown to others.

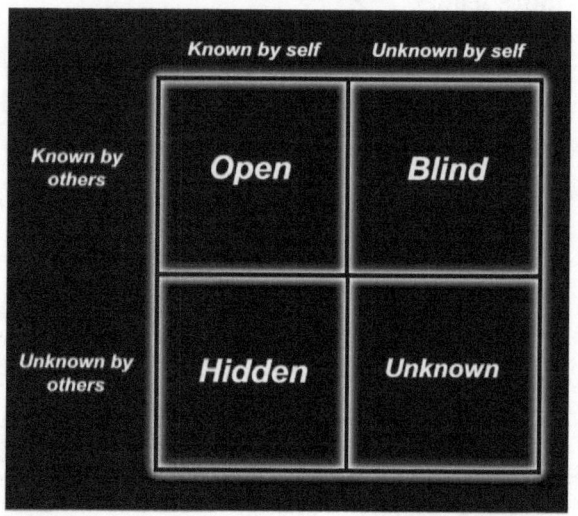

People often know the world, or only know themselves. To successfully lead your life one must know self but also the world to be able to exercise choices that take them closer to their desired life.

Nick: Does that mean we may tend to become a copy of the kind of people that we are surrounded with, unless we know our true self. But then why are we afraid of what we are meant to be?

Roy: Yes! We are often afraid of failure as well as success?

Nick: I can understand the fear of failure but why are we scared of success?

Roy: You have actually answered the question that we all fear failure, so we have subconsciously identified fear as our permanent enemy. Since we have identified fear as our enemy, as and when it surfaces we want to fight it out. Same is our reaction when we are close to success. We fear anxiety when we are close to success and sometimes behave as if we are in any a fearful situation leading to sabotaging our success.

The best part is, more often, we are completely unaware that we are doing that to ourselves.

Nick: You mean reacting negatively when we are close to success!

Roy: True! Often our conditioning is responsible for believing that:

- Some of us have been made to believe by naysayers that we are mediocre and don't deserve success.

- Some shy and introvert people may shirk away from limelight and success.

- Some people get so comfortable in their status quo life that they dread leaving it even for success.

- Some of us, who have faced certain emotional traumatic experiences in the past, may connect the anxiety of success with same traumatic experience and hence sabotage our success.

- Some people connect success with competition, which they hate; they feel they may displease someone.

- Some don't feel safe being successful as this will not be as per the expectations of those who have surrounded them for years.

- Some feel that on coming into the limelight, people will ridicule and pull them down hence they avid coming in lime light.

- No one will judge me if I am not visible; if I get too visible because of success people will judge me and may ridicule or criticize me.

Nick: I just checked, fear of success is termed as Achievemephobia!!

Roy: Those suffering from that often achieve success and still throw it away by acting in a manner which is against their normal behavior. This is just because they are holding a certain picture of someone in their mind, who is someone mediocre, a struggler and non-deserving of success.

Fear can be motivating for some and discouraging for some. It depends on how we respond. For that, we could try positive visualization and change our image from someone fearful to someone confident and successful.

Roy: The discovery of becoming one's best version is achieved often through introspection leading to freedom of choice and for some it is an impactful event that becomes a cause of discovery for what they are meant to be. Introspection leads to improved self-control.

Nick: Self-control is the ability to control self-behavior in terms of emotions, actions, thoughts etc during trying situations.

BEWARE OF FEAR
IT KILLS MOST DREAMS

"We can easily forgive a child who is afraid of the dark; the real tragedy of life is when men are afraid of the light."

– Plato

Plato was an Athenian philosopher in Ancient Greece, founder of the Platonist school of thought, and the Academy, the first institution of higher learning in the Western world.

Roy: The following poem by Marianne Williamson inspires & introspects Fear

Our deepest fear is not that we are inadequate.

Our deepest fear is that we are powerful beyond measure.

It is our light, not our darkness that most frightens us.

We ask ourselves wrong questions:

Who am I to be brilliant, gorgeous, talented, and fabulous?

Am I shining too bright and should I tone done my brilliance to fit with everyone?

The right thoughts are: You are a child of God.

Your playing small does not serve the world.

There is nothing enlightened about shrinking so that other people will not feel insecure around you.

We are all meant to shine, as children do.

We were born to make manifest the glory of God that is within us.

It is not just in some of us; it is in everyone and as we let our own light shine, we unconsciously give others permission to do the same.

As we are liberated from our own fear, our presence automatically liberates others.

Nick: Why is fear is such a barrier to achieving Leadership vision?

Roy: According to Beaulieu (1999) "it is possible that a person's fear of failure or rejection can be stronger than his need for achievement or status"

If a leader's fear is more than his courage to succeed, he will simply not move to take enough initiative to start a project, forget sustaining it. Fear can hold people prisoners for life without them ever knowing that they have lived a life in prison of fear.

Don't Be a Prisoner of Your Own Perceptions

Nick: Because of some herd mentality or some irrational fear!

Roy: There is nothing more tragic then realizing at the end of the life I should have done that or why didn't I try pursuing the passion of my life!! Often these rational and irrational fears hold us hostage to taking a leap towards what we always wanted to do.

Nick: Types of fear that leaders have to face:

- Fear of Failure!

- Fear of Criticism!

- Fear of getting judged!

- Fear of getting hurt!

- Fear of making a Wrong Decision!

- Fear of stepping in Uncertainty!

- Fear of Change & Discomfort!

- Fear of Rejection!

- Fear of not being good enough!

- Fear of being Left Alone!

- Fear of Missing out: "FOMO"!

- Fear of not knowing everything

- Fear of starting a Project

- Fear of Consequences!

Roy: Fear takes away the joy and happiness at work, when we work in organizations where leadership is based on creating a fearful environment we are robbed from being our best, we no longer feel empowered, we are not able to exceed expectations. **However as per Ferris (1998) contended that leaders fear more about safety of the people who they are responsible for, then fearing their personal fears.**

Nick: Let me also add, according to Suarez (1994)

"Fear erodes joy in work, limits communication and stifles innovation"

Nick: In such a situation a person becomes procrastinating and may stop taking actions towards his vision, hence falling short in his life in achieving much.

What are different responses to fear?

Roy: Some of the common responses to fear are:

- Fail to take any action

- Procrastinate

- Stay in denial of the situation

- Nervousness

- Inability to stay focused

- Feeling stressed

- Showing courage and grit to stand and face consequences

- Fight it

- Run away from the situation and not face the situation (taking a flight)

- Feeling motivated to fight

- Feeling de motivated

Roy: To defeat fear one has to understand fear better, for example fears can be classified in two types:

Rational Fear: Fearful event which is likely to happen or a fearful situation that is likely to appear

Irrational Fear: These are those fears which have no basis in reality yet we are afraid of these and are not likely to happen.

Nick: What you mean is Rational fears are more realistic and Irrational fears are basically unrealistic and imaginations of our over active brains, with almost no possibility of occurrence.

Attitude towards Fear was best described by:

Michel de Montaigne about 500 years ago said: (was one of the most significant philosophers of the French Renaissance, known for popularizing the essay **as a** literary genre)

"My life has been filled with terrible misfortune; most of which never happened."

Nick: That means that more than often our fears are baseless, and rarely, come true!

However let me also add what stress caused because of fear can lead to:

Lower IQ!

Anxiety!

Heart problem!

High Blood pressure!

Inaction!

Feeling Victimized!

Hence understanding failure and defeating failure is crucial to achieving personal as well as organizational goals.

Nick: How do effective leaders deal with fear?

Roy: Leaders understand that fear can be the biggest hindrance in their success.

- They know that preparation destroys fear

- Knowing more and preparing more makes fear diminish

- Visualization is another technique which is used by sports man to overcome fears.

- Taking action in spite of fear puts fear in its place.

- Visualization is imagining/or painting a clear picture in our mind of a positive outcome of our enterprise.

Even though everyone wants to succeed in life yet most choose to continue being in their comfort missing what they do the best. Not leaving the comfort zone in life is a reason because of which majority of people don't take the uncharted road to success as they fear unknown situations and circumstances. Hence most don't even start and continue living life as it comes.

Nick: You mean they live a life of default?

Roy: The difference between a life of design and life of default is courage.

In the absence of courage fear keeps them a prisoner throughout their lives and they continue sleep walking only to avoid some unknown fears which control their lives

Nick: Isn't that tragic! What is the price they pay of not facing fears?

Roy: The price of not facing our fears in our lives is huge. The price is regret when one's life comes to an end they regret they could have done so much more in their life and wonder why they worried, as most of the things they feared never happened throughout their lives

Nick: You mean most of the fears are just unrealistic, baseless and never happen. Also fear leads to more fear and issues like anxiety and inactiveness creep into personality which further spiral down one's life. Whatever we practice grows; if we assume being in a fearful state mostly, it keeps growing and starts controlling us.

Roy: Very true but the price we have to pay in our lives because of not facing them with courage is huge

Nick: What do you mean by "Paying a Huge Price?"

The Huge price we pay for living fearfully all our life are the following:

- We don't live the life of purpose we always wanted to live

- We are unable to be decisive as fear takes charge of our life

- It robs us of unlimited life opportunities which we are fearful to try

- Fear makes one's life struck

- Fear holds our progress and growth and stops us from becoming our best selves

Fear leads to paralysis of analysis and makes one inactive and confused which ultimately leads to despair and feeling as a victim. Feeling fearful during threatening situation is a natural response which is designed by nature.

Nick: How to leaders react when they face fear

Roy: No one can escape coming face to face with fear!

Leaders must face fear and deal with it directly. To tackle fear we must understand fear. As research proves that we are born with just two fears one is fear of falling and second fear of loud noise. Rest all other fears we learn as we grow. We learn these fears from people around us, if a parent is fearful of swimming he hands over that fear to his kids too. If a grandparent has been preaching not to talk to strangers, than that fear of strangers is handed over to kids, from one generation to others.

Nick: So we develop more and more fears than we are actually afraid of. The world makes us fearful at every step rather than making us courageous.

Some of the fears that we all face:

- Fear of insignificance
- Feeling of ill health
- Fear of a death of a loved one
- Feeling of Poverty
- Fear of felling left out in the community
- Fear of an uncertain future, so in short no one can escape fear.

Nick: I have always wanted to understand courage and grit more!

As per Marriam-Webster dictionary Courage means

"**Strength of mind to carry on, in the face of danger or difficulty**"

As per Merriam-Webster dictionary Grit Means

Firmness of mind or spirit: Unyielding courage in the face of hardship or danger

Grit was defined as "perseverance and passion for long-term goals" by psychologist Angela Duckworth and colleagues, who extensively studied grit as a personality trait. (*Angela* Lee *Duckworth* (born 1970) is an American academic, psychologist and popular science author).

Roy: Those who had grit were able to stay courageous for longer period of time. Grit is one of the characteristics which leaders must have to see through failure. Courage does not mean you are not afraid, it means in spite of being afraid you keep moving ahead.

Roy: One of the key roles of the leaders is to fight fear with courage not only in their personal development and decision making but also to nurture a work culture devoid of fear in the organization.

The organizations that are driven based on fear have disengaged and disconnected employees who are not aligned with the company objective and goals. Fear driven organizations show low productivity and morale of a team.

Nick: But are leaders never fearful, how is it that they don't fear under stressful and volatile situations?

Roy: I firmly believe that it is only human to be fearful sometimes however facing it boldly and by taking action in that direction one feels in control. A leader may display some fear while facing it with courage, builds trust and shows they are authentic.

Nick: How do leaders tackle fear?

Let us understand that fear can have a crippling effect! It has a lot to do with our concept of fear we carry in our mind. Let me share some findings by Charles Darwin

Charles Darwin carried out a highly nonscientific test on himself during a visit to the London Zoological Gardens in 1872.

"I put my face close to the thick glass-plate in front of a puff adder... with the firm determination of not starting back if the snake struck at me," he later wrote. "But as soon as the blow was struck, my resolution went for nothing, and I jumped a yard or two backwards with astonishing rapidity. My will and reason were powerless against the imagination of a danger which had never been experienced."

Charles Darwin asked himself why he was behaving like that, and he came to a conclusion that was like that because of what all he had learnt & was told about snakes in his entire life & that has been his mental conditioning.

To deal with fear we may have to do a lot of unlearning about our concept of fear! To deal with fear we have to revisit the concept of fear which we have learnt since our birth.

Roy: It is essential that fear must be confronted to lead from the front. Fear is a kind of a warning that one has to be cautious and careful. Fear also signifies that we are moving out of our comfort zone. We should be watchful about the difference between rational and irrational fears. Our focus needs to be on what we want to happen and not on what is worst that could happen and engage with our subconscious mind and communicate the same, which is called visualization technique. Yet be mentally prepared to overcome the worst possible outcome!

Break down fear in to smaller parts! Courage destroying fear examples are all around us, patients fighting life threatening diseases, old age people living alone, single parent, etc are present all around us. Let us identify what are the symptoms of a fear based organization! Some of the characteristics are:

• Lack of accountability

• Distrust

• Making lame excuses

• Blame game and pass the buck attitude

• High employee turnover

• The rule of the organization is do or get punished

• Missing honest feedback

• Constant fear of job

• Workforce feel constant anxiety

• The focus is to maintain status quo

• Focus is to finish one's own job only to avoid punishment or reprimand

Nick: What are the characteristics of a Courage based organization?

Courage based organizations have clarity that is based on the values and vision of the company. Everyone serves the purpose and not just to please the boss.

Leaders often master the outer leadership competencies as they get paid for that behavior. In this race to compete in leadership with others leaders forget to develop inner character traits. Small undeveloped flaws in character may lead to troubled relationships and trust issues in the team. As leadership is an inside out job, one cannot fake leadership for long. Leaders must be authentic and their day to day behavior must be trustworthy and respectable for others to believe them. If the leaders show courage and values towards the organization the team inculcates that behavior and establishes it as a culture. The organizational values should be visible in the day to day behavior of the leadership.

Some of the characteristics of Organization based on Courage:

- Empowered team members to take decisions

- Culture of mutual respect, empathy and collaboration

- Aligned efforts of the organization towards the purpose and not the centralized authority

- Open communication

- Happy employees with high morale and motivation

- Strong trust amongst team members and good collaboration

- Encouragement to continuous improvement and change for better

- Accepting failure and mistakes as part of the growth.

- Emphasis on continuous learning & development of the organizational leaders and team members

- Fair methods of recognition and rewards

- Clear goals & vision.

FAILURE IS A GREAT TEACHER

"If you fail, never give up because F.A.I.L. means
"First Attempt In Learning"; End is not the end,
if fact E.N.D. means "Effort Never Dies,"

Avul Pakir Jainulabdeen Abdul Kalam was an
aerospace scientist who served as the 11th President
of India from 2002 to 2007

Nick: What is the difference between the amateur
and a professional expert?

Roy: Professional expert is the one who keeps
training inspite of repeated failure and the
amateur gives up after experiencing few
failures.

Everyone faces failure in their lives but it
is the attitude towards failure that defines a
leader. Leaders are not scared of facing failure
however losers are scared of failing. Hence
losers play it safe and never give it a try.

Nick: Attitude of Michael Jordan towards failing:

"I've missed more than 9000 shots in my career. I've lost almost 300 games. 26 times I've been trusted to take the game winning shot... and missed. I've failed over and over and over again in my life. That is why I succeed."

– Michael Jordan

Difference between an amateur and professional is of habits and discipline. Any Professional sports person works hard and sticks to discipline and an everyday practice regime that keeps him at the top of his game. Discipline is hard & it is about showing up for practice daily. It is about committing to get better and better. It is about sticking to the practice schedule and diet discipline etc even though one hates to do that.

Amateur practice to get it somewhat right and are extremely happy to have achieved that mediocre level

Professional practice until they get it always right

Professional world class athlete's train so hard that there performance does not change even if there are some variables. For example a Champion tennis player like Roger Federer, Nadal or Djokovich there performance does not change if even if there is any of the below variables:

- If it gets too windy

- If the crowd is hostile

- If the match is scheduled in natural light or artificial light

- If the match is played during day or during night

- If it is too humid

That actually means that they have trained well not only physically but also mentally and emotionally well to face and withstand any changes and deliver consistent performance no matter what changes.

However on the other hand an amateur would lose his cool if there is a small tiff with the umpire or because of a bad start or may be a little hostile crowd or extra heat or may be as simple as a bad night sleep. This also applies in life, most of the people live life like an amateur and few lead like professionals.

AMATEUR

PROFESSIONAL

AMATEUR	PROFESSIONAL
Wants to be noticed	Aims to be remembered
Have inconsistent Performance	Have consistent Performance
Focus on short term achievements	Focus on long term achievements
Give up at the first sign of failure	See failure as opportunity to grow and get better
See feedback as criticism	See feedback as identification of weak spot
Have a goal	Have a process to achieve the goals
Enjoy doing fun part of the task	Committed to all parts of the task (easy & difficult)
They practice when they feel like it	They practice as a habit even if they don't feel like doing it
Stop when they achieve something	Keep going as they know this is just the beginning
Amateurs blame others	Professionals take responsibilities

AMATEUR	PROFESSIONAL
Practice for fun and enjoyment	Recognize that results in practice are same as results in an actual game.
Do not prepare to win, prepare to have fun	Prepare to win and excel
Look for validation from others	Strong self-belief
Focus on the outcome and not the process	Focus on work and give best effort
Try to get pass ahead without mastering the technique	Apply themselves to master the technique
Give up when they face setbacks and start doubting self	Face major setbacks and defeats yet keep moving ahead

Nick: Isn't failure inevitable when leaders set out on a new path chasing ambitious goals?

Roy: Failure strikes because in spite of the best of planning some road blocks appear which no one is prepared to handle. That actually requires a clear mind set, which means we need to have a fresh look, a new way to solve that.

No one can escape failure in some form or the other moving ahead in unknown future. Leaders don't take failure personally, as they completely understand that failure is a journey to success! It is like the concept of net worth and self-worth. Often self-worth goes down when someone suffers a financial loss. But it is actually a financial loss only and not a personal loss, same is failure. It is just an event or an attempt that has failed and not the person.

Leaders never take failure personally and keep moving ahead.

Roy: Don't you want to add the quote from your favorite movie *Rocky?*

Nick: I was about to.

"It isn't about how hard you hit. It's about how hard you are hit and keep moving forward"

– Rocky Balboa (Rocky Movie-starring Sylvester Stallone)

We will all be hit badly in our life with a blow which will bring us down, what life lesson can we learn from boxing is that no matter how hard we are hit, we need to get up and be ready to move on and not stay down.

Roy: Failure is a constant companion to success. Failures teaches us more than success does, as a matter of fact facing failure and keeping going is one a crucial trait of leadership. As research shows that 90% of the businesses fail in the first five years.

Nick: What are some of the reasons for that?

Some of the common reasons to hit failure are:

- Lack of clear vision or purpose

- Lack of taking big action which leads to no progress status, which further leads to lower morale.

- Lack of courage and grit to carry on through difficult times

- Loss of self-belief and self-confidence when one meets failure

- Self-sabotaging – whereby one doubts one's capability and confidence to achieve goals

- Trying to survive and succeed only on the basis of talent and not investing in self-development

- Low Productivity

- Teams that are not aligned and motivated towards the vision.

- Not having developed a process to conduct business

A combination of the above is a sure way leading to failure.

"Success is the ability to go from one failure to another without loss of enthusiasm."

– Winston Churchill

(Sir Winston Leonard Spencer-Churchill was a British politician, army officer, and writer. He was Prime Minister of the United Kingdom)

"Winners are not afraid of losing. But losers are. Failure is a part of the process of success. People who avoid failure also avoid success."

– Robert T. Kiyosaki

(Robert Toru Kiyosaki is an American businessman and author of Rich Dad Poor Dad)

Nick: I got this, let me draw this:

TRY – FAIL – TRY AGAIN – KEEP TRYING – SUCCESS

Nick: I get that now, let me add another quote:

"You lose 100% of the shots you don't take."

– Wayne Gretzky

(Wayne Douglas Gretzky CC is a Canadian former professional ice hockey player and former head coach. He has been called "the greatest hockey player ever")

Roy: So as leaders we must take our shots and not stay down for long even when we miss an aim, the game is not lost. The response to missing an aim is to prepare more and take a better shot next time.

Nick: You mean that leaders have failed more than those who never started, and that is what makes them an expert.

Roy: Failure teaches Leaders in various ways and prepares them for bigger challenges.

Failure teaches the following:

- It fine tunes the art of survival.

- It pushes one to reinvent themselves as a person or may be relooking at the process which failed.

- It helps understand what works and what does not.

- It's a signal that the course needs a correction of direction or action.

- Failure helps leaders understand humility.

- If there are no failures it reflects leaders are not trying hard enough.

- Failure teaches leaders to be more resilient.

Also most of the time we are more afraid of the fear of failure than the actual failure, that phobia of failure in some distant future has a crippling effect and imprison's one not to take any action.

Leaders must be prepared emotionally to handle failure. There is in fact no true story of huge success which is exempt of failure.

Nick: How do Leaders face failure?

Roy: Let me sum it how leaders work while facing failure:

- Not taking failure personally as it is only a way that has failed not the person

- Not to pay any attention or worry about the judgment, of people who never dared

- They learn and adapt from the failure and get better

- And apply principle used by Don Shula-Head Coach Miami Dolphin-Lead to the only perfect season in the History of National Football League (NFL)

(The rule that is to have a 24 hour rule: Policy of looking forward, and would allow himself and his team only to regret and rejoice a failure/victory for only 24 hours only & prepare to move ahead.)

Roy: They face failure by staying true to the purpose and by staying focused:

- They don't try and overlook facts because of their false ego.

- They continue communicating with their team to find solutions.

- They don't dwell in failure and don't let it pull them down.

- They don't panic and take hasty measures.

- They take accountability for the failure and not blame others

- Maintain morale of the team to continue finding out solutions to turn around the situation.

Leaders must examine their roots/relationship with fear.

Leaders control failure by preparing and knowing more about a situation.

"I believe that anyone can conquer fear by doing the things he generally fears to do, provided he keeps doing them until he gets a record of successful experience behind him."

– Eleanor Roosevelt

(Anna Eleanor Roosevelt was an American political figure, diplomat and activist. She served as the First Lady of the United States)

It is important that we understand failure and its root for example

- Procrastination

- Competency issue

- Lack of Determination

- Lack of Self Confidence

- Poor Self Image

Roy: Leaders ensure that failing is normal; it's a part of success achieving process. The organizations which stay ahead provide an environment to innovate for the teams trying new ideas that involve risk. The target is to succeed but in case it they face failure the leaders support those who tried!

For example Richard Branson started over 100 businesses.

Sir Richard Branson (is a businessman & investor, author and philanthropist. Started Virgin Group in the 1970s, has overseen approx 500 companies)

Yet there have been some failed businesses but that did not stop Sir Richard to stop innovating as an entrepreneur. Some of the failed businesses have been:

Virgin Cola-Virgin Cars-Virgin ware-Virgin Vodka-Virgin Digital Student Magazine-Virgin Brides-Virgin clothing

Nick: You mean if leaders do not support innovative ideas and risks, the team would shirk away from innovation and do as per their defined job profiles only and would stop innovating. Also this makes leaders more authentic and emotionally closer, leading to a stronger bond with the team. When a leader works with a team to come out of failure and encourage them to try again to work better they earn higher trust and loyalty of the team

Roy: Leaders who are credible are believed, trusted and followed more. By credible, I refer to those leaders who take responsibility for their risk and if failed stay accountable for the same, rather than shirking, ignoring failure or blaming others.

Failing is a step towards innovating and learning, what does not work, and step up the game to get better. Not innovating and not taking risks is a zero failure attitude and staying in the safe zone. But this is a zone of status quo which means not growing! This puts organizations at a greater risk where by their competition can easily defeat or overtake them by reinventing and taking risks.

Some of the businesses which failed to innovate as they believed that their success would continue the same way as it has been in the past. For example brand Nokia which deteriorated from the being the leader across the world in 2007 to losing everything by 2013. The down fall can be attributed to

- Lack of innovation
- Rigid management & -Lack of vision

TRUST CONSTITUTES THE CORE OF LEADERSHIP

Roy: Trust is the building block of any relationship. No effective collaboration can take place in absence of trust. It is Trust that converts a group into a team. There exists a very strong connection between leadership and trust. Trust is that special invisible bond which keeps the leaders and the followers together. Leaders believe in long term success and not short term profit. Key role of leaders is to:

- Achieve the vision
- Take big action towards it
- Align the team to perform towards shared vision.

Nick: And without trust none of the above can be accomplished.

Roy: Let me share tangible benefits of trust. Warren Buffet's example when his company invested in Walmart, is a great example which was also mentioned in one of the letter to shareholders from Berkshire Organization. In one of the investment made by Warren Buffet in Walmart which was called McLane deal. The investment meeting lasted around 2 hours and the entire deal investment took less than a month to complete.

An investment which would have otherwise taken almost a year or more for conducting due diligence before investing, was completed in less than a month. This was possible because both the organizations were operating on the basis of trust.

"Trust is like air we breathe. When it is present, nobody really notices. But when it is absent everybody notices."

– "Warren Buffet"

Things move at a much faster pace in an environment of trust and also cost lesser. For example in the case study of investment by

Warren Buffet, it was not only executed faster but also was cost effective as minimal time in due diligence was spent as both the parties were having a background of strong ethics and trust.

Let us take an example of airlines check in procedure, it used to be faster few years before but the worldwide increase in terrorism, smuggling and aircraft highjacks broke that trust worldwide leading to stricter checking norms leading to slower process and increasing the overall costs.

The latest loyalty driver worldwide of customers is, whether they can trust a particular brand or not. Not only customer, but to secure a culture of trust, organizations hire people who can be trusted. Once trust is established operating becomes smooth and efficient

Environment of trust gives better results as people are happier to collaborate and achieve a win-win situation rather than being competitive at all times. Trust avoids over supervision and micro management. It is based on empowering the front line which improves the bottom line

Google is one of the most valued, innovative Organizations of our times! The following is said by Sergey Brin, Co-founder and CEO of Google has to say about trust and its importance:

"We wouldn't survive if people didn't trust us," **"Obviously everyone wants to be successful, but I want to be looked back on as being very innovative, very trusted and ethical and ultimately making a big difference in the world."**

Nick: Is there any financial impact of trust?

Roy: In the absence of trust the cost of operations goes high and also the speed gets slower. For example if the trust of a customer goes down he wants to know more and more about the purchase and wants to cross check every information being provided and hence his process of making a decision is slowed down. In any organization if the trust is low, then everyone passes the problem and no one is ready to take any action or ownership as all of them feel they will end up blaming each other.

At airports around the world if we see, because of growing terrorism it now takes series of pre boarding checking of the passengers and the list of do's and don'ts have fairly increased. The pre boarding time required to reach the airport has increased for the passengers around the world and so is the cost to manage procedures of extra checking and vigilance at the airport.

Some of the benefits of companies with a trusted work culture are:

- Higher Profits

- Increased productivity

- Increased Employee morale

- Higher employee retention.

- Competitive market advantage

- Higher trust of customers on company and products

- Increased customer loyalty and promoters in the marketplace

A leader either leads on basis of fear or on basis of trust.

Trust based leadership beats the fear based leadership always

Leadership where the team fears the leader and find him to be unapproachable and fail to deliver. This style of leadership is based on leaders own fears and insecurities. However a trust based leadership, where the leader is available, approachable, listens, has time and works to facilitate effective solutions for the team. A leader, who shows a great amount of empathy, is able to see where the shoe hurts for his team and what issues are stopping them from achieving the goals, thus has an opportunity to act as a catalyst in destroying their fears and ends up being respected, trusted and followed. Fear could be a great barrier to innovation and moving ahead confidently.

Nick: So a trusted environment also fuels innovation as the members are not afraid to innovate and fail while trying as they feel secure. This develops a sense of belonging for the organization.

Nick: Are you trying to say that one cannot be a leader without trust?

Roy: Completely True! If people don't trust a leader, no results can be achieved. Trust is that key factor!

Nick: Are we not living in a world where trust is diminishing?

Trust diminishes when leaders show following behavior:

- When they make false commitments!

- When they do not communicate clearly

- When their intentions are to make certain employees fail

- When they do not share any credit for the work done

- When they micro manage everyone and do not empower

- When their attitude is of a fault finder only

- When they pretend they care

How do leaders build trust?

Roy: Trust is not something which can be built overnight it has to be built over a period of time. Leaders also have the responsibility to be trust worthy.

Roy: Leaders built trust with teams by:

- Demonstrating expertise in judgment

- By staying consistent in their behavior

- Helping team members succeed

- Giving honest feedback

- Treating with respect and care

- By being fair in their day to day behaviour

- By appreciating and sharing credit for good work

Nick: Means they should be worthy of trust of the followers!

Roy: In order to be trust worthy, leaders should be authentic and credible. They should display respect and fairness in there interaction and dealings with their team members. They should avoid favoring any particular team member.

Essence of Trust is when a work or task or responsibility can be delegated in full faith, with the belief that it will be done as you said. It is about keeping promises both small and big. It also refers that one would look after the interest of the other party without having been asked to do that. It means that you care about the other person well-being always.

Before leaders are trusted they have to ensure that they are actually trustworthy i.e. worthy of the trust of those who follow them. The trust building happens through effective interpersonal communication and multiple interactions over a considerable period of time.

Trust building is not achieved overnight it's a time taking process. It has to be earned step by step. Just because someone has a senior designation does not make him entitled for trust of his team members.

Nick: But who can be trusted?

Roy: Let me quote to explain that:

> "Whoever is careless with the truth in small matters cannot be trusted with important matters."
>
> – Albert Einstein

LEADERS MUST BE TRUSTWORTHY

Nick: Leaders must be credible! Can you help me understand that better?

Roy: Credible leader: needs to display the following qualities:

1. Consistent in their behavior: Credible leaders are competent and deliver results consistently. They show it in their behavior, may be to a level of being predictable and not changing their leadership styles often. They do what they say they will do.

2. Trustworthy leaders are responsive which means they are accessible and respond to the followers

3. They don't talk the walk but actually walk the talk.

Nick: Let me understand:

> **Talk the Walk**: Is when there is a difference between what a leader talks and what he actually projects in his day to day behavior.
>
> Vs
>
> **Walk the Talk**: that means that they lead by example, they show behavior and actions which they want the teams to follow. In short their behavior and words match up

Nick: They should also avoid the halo and the horn effect as this could be a barrier to trust building?

Roy: Will you please elaborate on halo and horn effect?

Nick: The Halo effect was first described in 1920 by psychologist Edward Thorndike in his paper titled "A Constant Error in Psychological Ratings." Halo effect is when once a positive image of a product or person is formed all other negative interactions in future are ignored.

> On the other side Horn effect is just the opposite of this, whereby a negative image of a product or a person, once formed continues to prevail as negative in spite of the future positive interactions.

Roy: Marketing and Advertising companies leverage this concept often in their marketing campaigns! For example if one of their product campaigns has been successful and popular they come out with more campaigns on the same lines leveraging the positive sentiments towards the company products. Buyers feel if one product of that company has been good and successful all others would be on the same lines as well.

LEADERSHIP AND MANAGEMENT ARE THEY SAME?

Management is efficiency in climbing the ladder of success: leadership determines whether the ladder is leaning against the right wall

– Stephen Covey

Nick: How is Leadership & Management Different?

Roy: Lets try and understand that from your perspective, since you do lot of trainings. How do you feel working with managers and working with leaders?

Nick: When I meet seasoned leaders they meet me with so much respect, they pay undivided attention and listen patiently and sometime even open the door and see me off.

Roy: So it sounds more like when you meet leaders they make you feel important & valued however managers feel they are important. It is a process managers get groomed into great leaders. Let us try and understand the essence of management and leadership. However Leaders may be acting like managers and managers may be great leaders in any organization. We will uncover all this as we proceed.

Let us try and list some differences between leadership and management!

LEADERSHIP

- Leaders challenge status quo & innovate

- It is about inspiring

- It is about vision & strategies

- Has a pull approach

- Ensure right things are done timely

- **Leaders work on the business

- Works to align people and teams

- It is about taking ownership

- Focuses on procedure

- Shapes culture

** Working in Business: Is that you are busy doing day to day work in the business

**Working on Business: Is about investing time and energy to build business for tomorrow.

MANAGEMENT

- It is about maintaining status quo

- It is about directing

- It is about operational thinking

- Has a push approach

- Ensure things are done the right way

- **Managers work in the business

- Busy organizing people

- Takes responsibility

- Focuses on policies

- Enacts Culture

**Working in Business: Is that you are busy dong day to day work in the business

**Working on Business: is about investing time and energy to build business for tomorrow.

WHY LEADERSHIP MATTERS

An expert in leadership Warren Bennis said,

"A business short on capital can borrow money and one with poor location can move but a business short on leadership has little chance of survival."

Roy: It is the most influential and critical element of all businesses. Organizations change with change in leadership, making it the single most important factor towards making or breaking an organization. Same businesses with same teams perform differently under different leaders. Effective leaders have the necessary tools and skills to inspire and encourage their teams allowing firms to run competently and smoothly. As a good leader, one should understand the mission statements, objectives, actions plans and goals of the company to be able to lead the workforce into realizing them.

The leader who made a difference alone is thing of the past. Today the business world is full of challenges and opportunities. The constant changes in business environment and technology today are something that a leader single handed cannot manage. Hence leaders must collaborate with the team to create innovations, achieve outstanding results and goals.

Roy: Hence the importance of leadership is very crucial.

They must work to bring out the best from the team members, keep the team together and motivated towards the objective. In these times leaders have to constantly adapt and innovate there game

New and innovative ways of doing business are making survival of traditional business difficult

Leaders must have the ability to be able to analyze and challenge their own personal and business practices on a regular basis rather than sitting tight on the past achievements. Leadership roles today have to be agile and not rigid and be able to see their businesses from their customers view point.

By knowing there market place in which they operate they must be able to anticipate the next upcoming challenge, change or opportunity well in advance and prepare accordingly by staying agile. This anticipation is a great advantage in the field of business, sports or personal life. Looking and thinking ahead with certainty is a leadership advantage.

So they must keep investing in their own learning continuously. Since leaders are so often busy pursuing targets and results they miss out developing and updating self.

Nick: But isn't the availability of so much data and information makes their job and decision making easier?

Roy: In fact they are flooded with so much of information on a daily basis from so many channels that it is easy to get misled. However leaders must be able to take decisions in spite of ambiguity! Even if the data/information available does not make the situation clear, still they must take a decision as they dig out there emotional intelligence and by thinking critically about the situation they are in.

Leaders must be comfortable to adapt to a fast paced changing scenario for which they must be equipped with sound knowledge of the corporate world and changes that are taking place.

Leaders have to choose the best options amongst the maze of confusing choices which is an expert role. Since leaders carve a new path most of the people are unable to relate to them and often criticize them. Leaders are more in tune of their inner voice or purpose that propels them to achieve extraordinary goals. In a way they have unreasonable expectations from themselves and they are constantly keep raising the bar. They are flexible to learn a skill that is required for a particular task so they continuously keep learning. Leadership can be a game changer in personal as well as professional life.

Effective Leadership benefits to an organization are:

- Make better decisions

- Get more done in less time with lower costs

- Organizations achieve better results

- More engaged staff with the vision

- More trusted teams with high productivity

- Agility in the organization: which helps in dealing with disruptive market situations and competition

Roy: At the core of each achievement is leadership aimed at achieving a vision.

Leadership must establish a common purpose to achieve within a defined time line.

Along with creating a synergized team towards the goals/vision through communication of the goals:

- Create a shared vision

- Influence and Transform

- Break the status quo by innovating

- Providing direction in the new unexplored path ever before

- Anticipate obstacles and overcome them

- Create more leaders

- Achieve the vision

TRADITIONAL VS CONTEMPORARY MANAGEMENT

Nick: What is the difference between the traditional hierarchy model and the new model?

Roy: The new business hierarchy has inverted the pyramid. The reason for this is the following:

It makes the organizations more flexible and agile

Nick: The older version was slow and rigid

Roy: It adds value to the front line staff which makes them more engaged

The inverted model is based on empowered employee and moves away from the old style of micro-managing teams and giving directions at all times

Nick: Let me share the smallest rule book and a classic example of Upside down hierarchy model!

Nordstrom Employee Handbook — a single 5-by-8-inch card containing 75 words:

Welcome to Nordstrom. We're glad to have you with our company. Our number one goal is to provide outstanding customer service. Set both your personal and professional goals high. We have great confidence in your ability to achieve them. Nordstrom Rules: Rule #1: Use best judgment in all situations. There will be no additional rules. Please feel free to ask your department manager, store manager, or division general manager any question at any time.

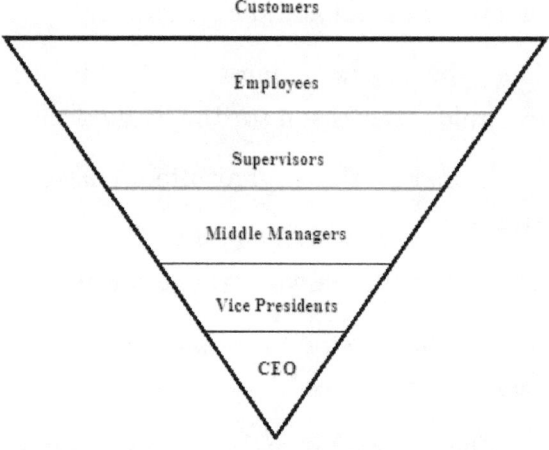

Inverted Hierarchy Pyramid In Organizations

It's a myth that by constantly telling people to move faster, move faster they will start moving faster, however the real speed will come only when leaders pay attention and commit to removing obstacles from the path of their teams process. This inverted pyramid is actually a result of this thinking. **The best leadership to support this is servant leadership whereby the leader is committed to serve the teams and is busy removing obstacles and empowers and coaches the team to work with confidence and authority.**

LEADERSHIP STYLES

The major weakness of style and behavioral theories is that they ignore the important role which situational factors play in determining the effectiveness of individual leaders (Mullins, 1999). There is often a debate that one style does not fit all situations.

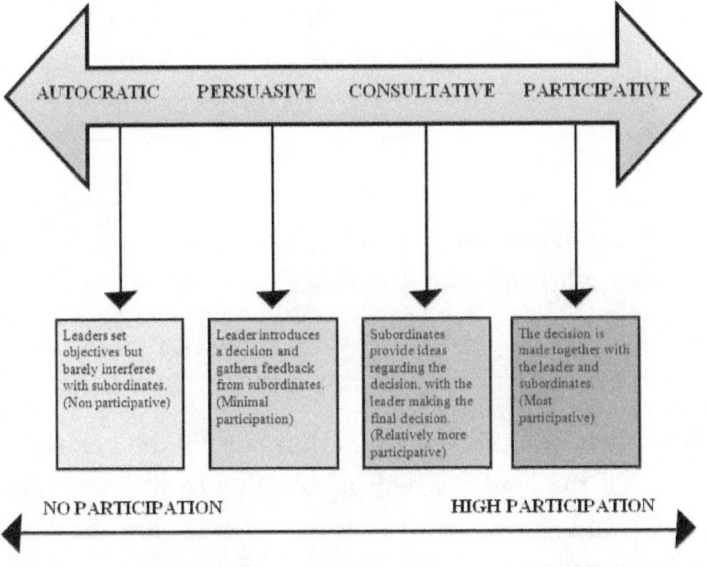

AUTOCRATIC	PERSUASIVE	CONSULTATIVE	PARTICIPATIVE
Leaders set objectives but barely interferes with subordinates. (Non participative)	Leader introduces a decision and gathers feedback from subordinates. (Minimal participation)	Subordinates provide ideas regarding the decision, with the leader making the final decision. (Relatively more participative)	The decision is made together with the leader and subordinates. (Most participative)

NO PARTICIPATION   HIGH PARTICIPATION

TRADTIONAL MODEL OF MANAGEMENT   **CONTEMPORARY MODEL OF MANAGEMENT**

LEADERSHIP IS ESSENTIALLY A BEHAVIOUR

"The highest type of ruler is one of whose existence the people are barely aware.... The sage is self-effacing and scanty of words. When his tasks are accomplished and things have been completed, all the people say is: we ourselves have achieved it"

> – Lao Tzu: Philosopher &
> Poet of Ancient China
> Lao Tzu wrote about leadership
> in the 5th century BC

"It is not positions which lend distinction to but men who enhance positions"

> – Agesilaus: Greek King

Roy: It is not about the position but it's the behavior of the leader which adds value to the position. And most of the time leaders are leading without any title.

Roy: Leadership is not a title or a designation it is rather a responsibility and a behavior. Mostly leadership is confused with someone who is heading a company. In fact for leadership there is no requirement of a designation. Designation only means a position achieved in hierarchy of an organization.

Leadership is not about having more power, authority, a plush office or a flashy designation; it is about responsibility, a behavior.

It is about a collective goal, it is about influence. Leadership is not about me, it is about we or us leveraging through people. It is about creating a shared identity. Leadership is all about influence and relationship and not about controlling. Once the goals are accomplished, the team feels they have done it. Leaders tirelessly work to safeguard their team and push them to achieve more & to do things beyond the ordinary. They inspire by being an example, work with team, share credit, take responsibility of consequences, face criticism, face fear, overcome failure, show resilience, courage and grit to emerge as a leader

One becomes a leader when one is able to influence a group of people to take action towards a shared vision or a goal.

Leadership is about influence which is achieved by building trust and deep rooted relationships.

Nick: Relationships are built on care and trust, so leaders are caring yet daring!

Roy: Very true at times – leaders care more about who they lead than about themselves which further makes them trust worthy.

"The key to successful leadership today is influence, not authority."

– Ken Blanchard

(Kenneth Hartley Blanchard is an American author. His extensive writing career includes over 60 published books, The One Minute Manager, has sold over 13 million copies)

Roy: Before we know leadership we must know what leadership is not?

Leadership is not having a fancy designation as a VP/GM; it is not an entitlement to lead.

Management does not mean leadership. It is about more about influence than about controlling.

Nick: Is there something like a fake, toxic or pseudo – leadership!

Roy: Yes there is! The following behavior falls under poor leadership behavior

To know leadership we should also know the behavior of Ineffective & Pseudo Leaders.

- Ambiguous communication
- Inconsistent in their behavior
- Leaders who don't have a clear vision or purpose
- Lack of empathy
- Slow to react
- Rigid and not flexible
- Self Interest higher than purpose or team efforts
- Egoistic
- Play favorites to those who pamper them
- Lack of transparency
- They have fear as a tool to manage the culture
- They play blame games when faced with failure
- They are happy an comfort in the status quo
- They do not collaborate or leverage team strength
- They feel they know it all

Roy: Often positions are confused with leadership!

Often we find leaders are not authentic and just enacting the leader position because they have a fancy designation. It is very common to find in organizations that people often trust and get influenced more by someone who has a lower rank or designation in the organization & has more followers and is immensely trusted as compared to the top most position or the so called leadership position.

Often the so called entitled leadership (as per the position in the company) commands to be served rather than playing, supporting, guiding and empowering his team.

Successful Leadership is mostly confused with an increased control over the organization and its people.

ANYONE CAN BE A LEADER

Roy: Leadership can be earned every day. It is not about how we have lived the past year; it is about how we behave and act today and now on. Becoming a CFO/CEO or starting your own venture is not the only measure of leadership. We have often been taught just one aspect of leadership that is to become some one important and powerful, which is pushing everyone in one race. Anyone can be a leader – someone who enjoys working as a manager, starting a career as an apprentice, working in a hotel laundry, serving in army, being a housewife raising a family with hard work and responsibility, serving different people in an airways, giving a gentle word of encouragement to someone feeling dejected. etc

Nick: Those who thanklessly work to face customers and bring a smile to their face create numerous moments of leadership which builds the world class leadership brands.

As a leader if we want to groom more leaders we need to be like pearl finders and not rag pickers

Nick: What does that mean?

Roy: It simply means as leader one should be on a look out to appreciate and encourage all the great small and big things teams are doing day in and day out. To be able to identify the leadership moments and them rather than staying busy with a fault finding attitude only. Leaders should not skip or miss such opportunities to appreciate as this forms the building block of the culture.

Also it is the responsibility of the leaders to develop values of integrity, mutual respect and accountability etc.

Nick: What is the relevance of spending time to develop these inner values?

Roy: These values bind the team and organization together. When everyone is driven by the same values it can be used in decision making as and when required. So even during the most of the difficult situation everyone is driven by these inner values and overcome difficult situations to stay empowered.

Roy: Let us not misunderstand leadership and simply aspire to be a leader who aims to only attain authority and power.

LEADERSHIP IS ABOUT TAKING INITIATIVE

Roy: The entire world looks upon leaders for this one key purpose, which is taking initiative. It is for this initiative that leaders are recognized and rewarded and admired. Leaders take initiative and confidently back it up with a plan and take concrete action to ensure that the initiative succeeds.

Nick: Initiative is about doing the right things even when we are not told to do that.

Roy: Leaders initiative is fuelled with so much passion and enthusiasm that it rubs on to others and more people buy that vision and get aligned with it. Leaders practice & display this trait & somehow attract others as well who want to develop these qualities in themselves as well and hence get aligned and trust the leader.

LEADERS HAVE A VISION

"Only thing worse than being blind is to have a sight but no vision."

– Hellen Keller

(Helen Adams Keller was an American author, political activist, and lecturer. She was the first deaf-blind person to earn a Bachelor of Arts degree)

Nick: Vision means that the leader has a clear goal and objective for himself and his team.

They cut out the distractions and confusion and avoid wasting time in being busy doing things which don't contribute to the final goal.

Roy: Being focused has the following advantages

- It helps being productive

- Reduced stress

- One moves faster and quickly towards the goals

- Subconscious mind gets activated and starts working leading to outstanding goals.

Leader knows the way ,
Goes the way & shows the way

Famous Quote by John C. Maxwell is an American author, speaker and pastor.

LEADERS MUST HAVE CLARITY OF PURPOSE

"Good business leaders create a vision, articulate the vision, passionately own the vision, and relentlessly drive it to completion."

– "Jack Welch"

(John Francis "Jack" Welch Jr. (born November 19, 1935) is an American business executive, author, and chemical engineer. He was chairman and CEO of General Electric between 1981 and 2001. During his tenure at GE, the company's value rose 4,000%.)

Roy: Vision is like a guiding light for leaders helping them to see where they are heading. Vision is kind of a conceptualized image of the future which is yet to take shape. It is a goal or a dream which a leader aims to accomplish along with his team. Vision is unforeseen future; hence leaders must prepare, plan and make changes to achieve it and stay relevant or ahead in the market place. Vision drives clarity and focus. This clarity helps in targeting concentrated action.

Nick: Does this focus bring in the concept of 80: 20 (Pareto's Principle)

Roy: Absolutely, vision is the guiding force to ensure that the leaders focus on vital few and not on inconsequential many. Vision gives a sense of purpose and meaning to their efforts which keeps them motivated and going

Nick: That means purpose not only drives them through difficult times but also motivates them to exceed their own expectations.

LEADERS ARE CURIOUS-
ASK QUESTIONS & LISTEN

Roy: Leaders are curious learners! They are always busy finding ways to do new or trying to work out old things in a better way. They are busy developing themselves, facing new challenges, taking risks, planning for future, investing in others. They know the danger of taking things for granted or sitting on old laurels. Old achievements do not guarantee future success. Leaders never stop learning and growing.

Nick: As well explained by Albert Einstein

"I have no special talent I am passionately curious"

Roy: Taking things for granted stops all learning and growth and that is when complacency seeps in. Leaders know the value of innovation and stay curious to look for better ways of doing things in a new manner. Leaders know very well that they do not know all, that makes them stay curious and this trait keeps them on their toes. They ask questions and the curiosity of their questions leads them to knowledge and innovation. That is what leads them to improved process and practices.

Leaders ensure to make listening as a top priority as that is how they get to know about people in their team, their ideas, concerns; etc as listening builds trust and relationships in an organization.

Some of the questions that leaders ask themselves all the Time:

- What are some of the barriers & obstacles that stop people from doing their best?

- What motivates team members?

- Are employee & organizational goals aligned?

- Do employee's feel empowered?

- Do employee's feel engaged & involved with the company?

LEADERS MUST INFLUENCE

As per the research by Rath, Conchie & Gallup Research Team, it was found that followers have four requirements to follow a leader (Study comprised of 10000 people in the role of a follower in the year 2009):

- Trust

- Compassion

- Stability

- Hope

Nick: Are there certain characteristic in leaders that followers look up to?

Roy: They expect the leader to be:

- A good listener

- The one who empowers and does not micro manage

- One who takes complete ownership of the consequences and does not play a blame game

- One who shows consistency in his action which is in tune with his values

- One walks the talk rather than not keeping his promises

- One who truly cares and is sincere and commited

They must be able to synergize the efforts of the teams completely with the vision

LEADERS VALUE HUMILITY

"Tibetans look at a person who holds himself above others, believing he is better than others and knows more, and they say that person is like someone sitting on a mountain top: it is cold there, it is hard, and nothing will grow. But if the person puts himself in a lower position, then that person is like a fertile field."

– Allan Wallace

Bruce Alan Wallace is an American author and expert on Tibetan Buddhism.

Roy: Ego of neither leaders nor followers should ever become a barrier in achieving objectives

Nick: I did hear somewhere the full form of ego?

Edge God Out

For those who exalt themselves will be humbled, and those who humble themselves will be exalted Christians read in Mathew 23:12

Ego for a leader could be a huge barrier as being full of pride; a leader starts to look down upon those who follow him and feels superior to them.

It's a fact that no one in this world knows everything and yet there is so much more that is still to be learned.

Roy: That is the beauty of this world that we can learn so much from each other all the time. Inflated egos stop leaders to collaborate and learn from others. Ego also stops leaders to leverage the collaborative intelligence of the team, making it weak. Inflated egos make leaders behave inappropriately with others, leading to breaking of trust, relationships and create unpleasantness and disrespect.

It also refers to refrain from judging others, leader is on a path to continuous progress & is open to ideas and suggestion to improve irrespective of who gives that suggestion and his rank or position dos not matter in the team.

Nick: But humility can easily be misinterpreted as weakness!

Roy: On the contrary humility is one of the biggest strength of the leaders! **True humility is when one has the capacity and courage to confront the situation but choose not to. It is not true humility when you lack the courage to confront and choose to go with the group because you do not want to be ridiculed or may be confronted. It is a choice that one makes to let go or ignore knowing well that one had the capacity to challenge and retaliate in that situation**

One of the crucial traits in effective leaders is they are humble. They know very well that they are not the smartest in the organization on all subject matters. Hence a humble leader is able to contribute more by leveraging the combine talent pool of the organization; however an egoist leader may completely miss out this aspect always believing that since he is positioned at the top of the hierarchy thus knows everything.

While recruitment of a CEO, this trait is generally overlooked in contrast to knowledge, experience, confidence, vision etc. But when taken a closer look we find that humility and empathy are closely linked. Humble and empathetic leaders are able to create more closely knit teams which are more productive. Humble leaders are great listeners and create an inclusive environment of respect, trust and security leading to great teamwork and performance.

Nick: Is this not moving towards servant leadership?

Roy: Often humble leaders are mistaken with weakness and there politeness is mistaken for being timid.

Servant leadership is when a leader is invisible and is not driven by external recognition, glory or fame. He is focused on serving his team to do better, provide them support and encouragement to excel. Such leaders respect and value everyone's contribution. They are kind, honest and fair in their leadership. They review the obstacles in the path of the teams and work tirelessly to remove those, by, training and coaching with their expertise. Since they are less distracted by external recognition they are able to focus more on the goals and how to achieve them. Since their behavior matches their talk, they also are easily approachable and are able to develop strong relationship with team based out of trust.

LEADERS SERVE THEIR TEAMS

Robert K. Greenleaf first coined the phrase "servant leadership" in his 1970 essay, "The Servant as a Leader."

LEADERS PUT TRUST AT THE CORE OF LEADERSHIP

Nick: They should be a role model as they are constantly under watch so they must walk their talk so that they can be trusted. There day to day behavior and interactions reveal their belief and values. To be trusted they must display honesty and integrity in their behavior on a daily basis! Do they behave respectfully and fairly with everyone or they are biased? If they are biased and disrespectful they can't be trusted or respected.

Roy: Trust of the employee is earned by an organization and is crucial for a business to succeed which is based on an employee's various moments' which are:

Are they being trusted?

Are they being heard?

Are they respected?

Are they being valued?

Are they being dealt fairly?

Nick: Moment of truth is a marketing term, which refers to whenever a customer comes in contact or experiences a product or service and establishes an opinion about the same. Similarly employees are our internal customers and every act of truth of the management must be positive and credible to establish a trusted work culture.

LEADERS BELIEVE IN NOT ONLY KNOWING BUT DOING

Roy: They understand the difference between movement and progress.

Nick: I am not sure I got that!

Roy: Some of us feel that moving around a lot being busy and running around all day we have accomplished a lot. **However it is not about running around and being busy, it is about what are we busy doing and what is the purpose and direction of our hard-work that defines our progress.**

Nick: And I learned earlier that leaders take big actions and never fall in the trap of procrastination or wanting to know everything & ending up over analyzing which is a trap, called paralysis of analysis

LEADERS HAVE A VOICE

Nick: What do you mean by that? Do you mean the tone, pitch or a style of speaking?

Roy: In fact what I meant was the voice of leadership signifies the values a leader stands for, however the pitch and tone do matter. **A polite and respectful communication gets better results than rude and insulting one.**

Roy: It is about the conviction that a leader has. **Leadership voice is what values a leader stands for.** It also means that they must have a clear stand in a particular situation which can only be achieved by understanding of the situation with courage. They have to know the environment they operate in, future trends of business as well as the team that they are managing and preparation to meet the future environment and expectations. **Leaders are not running to win a popularity election but they are the flag holders of the right voice, which gives the right direction in spite of the resistance.** Leaders feed their inner voice as they know that they are on a journey, to carve a path so they trust themselves and fuel their voice making it to be the loudest.

Nick: Do you also mean that while dealing with the team they should be able to put their point across directly and not dilute it as they want to be liked. Leaders are great communicators and they know talking straight with empathy works well.

Roy: True they are not in the business of getting popularity.

LEADERS SHOW POISE UNDER TROUBLED TIMES

Roy: Leaders are known to shine during troubled times. It is easier said than done facing troubled times! One cannot talk of leadership without reflecting on the trait of bouncing back!

Nick: Are you someway hinting at resilience?

Resilience has its roots from the Latin word word "resilire" which means leap back or recoil

Definition of resilience is the capacity to bounce back from a set back

Roy: That is one of the key learning's from sports where any game can turn around even from the last point depending on the ability of the sportsperson. There are numerous examples in almost every sport where teams and individuals have made come back from almost a lost spot to winning the game. And champions are those who have mastered the art of winning consistently no matter what the situation is!

In business there are numerous inspiring success stories where collapsed businesses have been developed into world class brands

And there are numerous icons of the world who in spite of their humble beginnings made impact on the world turning around there setbacks into success stories.

It makes easier to fight fear and face troubled times when the team facing that has faith and confidence in each other. It is in troubled time that leaders shine, as that is the time there courage and resilience is visible which commands respect from subordinates. By staying focused on the situation at hand and keeping the distractions and fear away, leaders win over the troubled times. It is the sense of purpose that helps them see through these times! Resilience includes mental physical and emotional balance. Emotional strength to carry on without feeling defeated or doubting self or feeling victimized

Nick: How important is physical strength to carry on in trying times?

Roy: If one is not physically fit and has a prolonged illness then it is even more challenging to recover from a setback. However, high energy and sound health levels support the emotional level to bounce back. They are committed to leverage the team strengths and inspire them to exceed their potential

Leaders are available and approachable

LEADERS LEVERAGE TEAM COLLECTIVE STRENGTH

You can do what I cannot do

I can do what you cannot do

Together we can do great things

Mother Teresa

Nick: Are leader's expert in dealing in all subjects?

Roy: I know this question is more to poke me rather than to know more as by now you know the answer very well. In today's competitive and complex business environment leaders have to use their skills of influence and persuasion to bring the team together. Leaders leverage the skills of various subject experts as they cannot be bogged down to micro managing tasks. Hence delegation and empowerment is the best way to achieve great results. **Infact an organizations true competitive power or advantage in the market lies in unleashing their talent pool which can work together leveraging each other strengths and achieve results. Today the problems and situations are so complex that it is not possible to solve them without involving those with expertise in the required domain.**

To achieve great and lasting results there is an essential requirement to collaborate & co-operate among teams. In the absence of co-operation no team can succeed or achieve their targets. So co-operation of the teams is essential to success. Leaders will fail if they cannot foster this feeling to co-operate or co-ordinate amongst teams. Leaders achieve this by fostering human element & moral compass across the organization which makes everyone collaborate. Getting a team together and to have them work in synergy is the expertise of the leaders.

A single man's achievements even if he is extremely talented and organized cannot match the productivity when collaborative efforts of synergized team come together. Team which win games win because of the team work and co-ordination and not because they have star's in their teams.

Nick: I am sure it is because of collaboration of people who are hardworking & sincere

Roy: Not only that, they must display trust, faith, sincerity & loyalty as success can only be built on these traits.

LEADERS MUST BE APPROACHABLE

Nick: Being approachable means being nice all the time?

Roy: Approachable means being available, giving time, talking with warmth and care. It does not mean that the leader is seeking attention or he wants to be liked or please his team! If a leader has a strong desire to be liked it starts affecting the performance and culture.

Approachable is a trait which makes his team members reach out to him for any requirement. It is the comfort and confidence a team member has in their leader that they would be given time and attention and will be heard patiently if they have a concern. Such leaders are consistent in their behavior, don't put other's down, show respect and do not over react to a trivial situation and show poise!

LEADERSHIP IS ABOUT STRAIGHT TALK

Nick: Some leaders are hesitant to share negative or constructive feedback, is that correct?

Roy: Leaders believe in straight talk which is honest and to the point so that it is well understood. They infact are more than willing to explain and repeat what they want to communicate so that it is clearly understood. Straight forward communication speeds up the process and makes the entire team more effective and productive. On the contrary when leadership communication or feedback is vague and lacks clarity that leads to an environment of distrust and confusion. It also in a way sends a message not to do straight talk as the leadership has set that tone in the organization.

Nick: What all a straight talk could be about?

Roy: Straight talk could be about clarifying one's role, clarifying organizational expectations from an employee, feedback about performance, behavior or attitude etc or may be aligning the teams with the vision.

LEADERS ADAPT-CHANGE AND RE-INVENT

Roy: Change is the only thing which is constant. Since there is no way to control the changing business environment what leaders do, is to equip and prepare themselves and the team to face the future challenges. When a company is small and in its initial phase the team and leadership are closely knit however as the number of people and business grows and some success is achieved, often the company slips into complacency & gets arrogant. Everyone starts feeling comfortable with the incoming customer response and profits and start believing that success would continue. This is the time when leadership must keep a close watch at the company culture and maintain open communication. Leaders must be connected with the team knowing what challenges they are facing and in turn the team members also must know what all is going on in the Company. Employees must be communicated openly about the organizational path, challenges and goals. This connection creates a clear shared vision and makes the company's agile to handle changes.

Nick: There is a famous Chinese quote which says that the wise adapt themselves to the circumstances as water adapt to the pitcher.

Can you please highlight what are the different aspects in which leaders must adapt?

Roy: Some of the adaptations required for leaders are:

- Open to accept new ideas and suggestions

- Evolve as per new situations and technologies

- To stay abreast with constantly changing business and work place environment

- Leaders don't let emotions cloud their vision

Nick: Are we talking about emotional intelligence?

Roy: Emotional intelligence is a facet of almost all effective leaders.

Nick: We are very much aware how un-controlled emotional outburst can disrupt relationships, teams, contracts, businesses and teams.

Roy: Leaders practice control and restraint from behaving rashly

Nick: Rash decisions or behavior may have painful results

Some of the rash behaviors are:

- Driving rashly out of rage

- Saying some extremely hurtful words out of anger

- Sabotaging or losing a business contract because of anger

- Losing a highly productive team member because of an uncontrolled situation

- Swaying away a from a discussion in a board meeting because of an ugly conflict

Roy: Leaders know the cost of harsh and reckless behavior hence they practice restraint and self-control. Emotions cloud vision leading to a distorted reality.

Nick: Do you mean leaders should be emotionless?

Roy: Not at all, they should rather show emotions but not let emotions rule their behavior. Leadership behavior is not driven by pleasing people but they are driven by purpose.

What I mean is that leadership should have emotional intelligence, which means they should be able to know their emotions and manage them well, rather than behaving like slaves to their emotions and mood.

Some of the practices emotionally intelligent leaders display

They respond to situations and not merely react

They always pause when they feel challenged to react and look at the bigger picture

They understand the importance of empathy and tone. Empathy helps leaders understand other person's point of view.

Nick: And the tone in which we speak is a major contributor to either escalating a conflict or defusing a conflict.

LEADERS SHOW THEY CARE

Nick: A caring leaders is one who shows interest in others. Caring leader is a concerned leader, who is sensitive towards the team!

Roy: A caring leaders is not only concerned about bigger things but is also aware of smaller things

Nick: Allow me to quote my favorite quotation by Maya Angelou

---

"I've learned that people will forget what you said, people will forget what you did, but people will never forget how you made them feel."

– Maya Angelou

Maya Angelou was an American poet, singer, memoirist, and civil rights activist.

Roy: Care is not something which one can fake; it is something which comes from the heart. It is extremely crucial to connect everyone together and to inspire and build trust. It is based on patience, kindness and being interested in the growth of the team as well as the individual members of the team

LEADERS MUST EMPOWER AND EMPATHISE

Roy: By empowerment I mean that the team must feel confident taking decisions. Often staff is trained on all policies and procedures. They are sure when to say no but they are not sure when to say yes if there is something beyond the defined company policy or procedures.

Nick: That means they are very clear about what all cannot be done as per the policies and procedures. They are well trained about what all to say "NO' to.

Roy: But they are not trained and empowered to say yes to what all which is not defined in the policy and procedures. Empowered employee's, are those who feel confident about taking decisions. They feel empowered by the trust and support of the management. They feel they will be supported for their decision making and not blamed. Leaders must foster an environment where people want to do things on their own and take decisions.

Nick: When someone takes a decision there is always a risk of making a mistake and sometimes the management reprimands with a job loss threat!

Roy: There lies the difference between a growth oriented leadership and stagnant outdated leadership. Leaders must empathize with their team to help them learn by giving them time, coaching and helping them grow. This attitude of developing more and more leaders is the key behavior of leadership. During such growth process leaders may come across as strict and demanding but in the bigger picture they are grooming mastery in their team. Leaders know well what a team is facing and going through as they perform there day to day tasks. Leaders are empathetic at heart, they are quick to assess when any policy or way of doing business is becoming complicated. They listen, observe and communicate openly with their team which helps them ascertain how the team feels and what is bothering them, which leads to changing process leading to an empowered and confident team.

Empowering is all about using the authority in a responsible manner.

LEADER'S SHARE & SERVE

Leaders share Vision

Leaders share Values

Leaders share Success

Leaders share their Time

Leaders share their Knowledge

Leaders share Accountability

Leaders share Culture

Leaders share Authority

Leaders share Rewards & Recognition

Leaders help clear obstacles from the path

Leaders serve their team to achieve greater heights

Leaders serve teams by day to day coaching

TOXIC LEADERS
SERVE-SELF

TRUE LEADERS
SERVE TEAM & VISION

LEADERS CREATE A PLAYFIELD INSIDE

Nick: How do you know that it's a great place to work at?

Leaders create an environment of growth. For example, just like plants grow in an environment of sunlight, air and water similarly, employees excel when they are trusted, valued & respected.

Nick: How does an employee know that he is in a great working environment?

Roy: By asking some simple questions one can ascertain that.

Let us look at some questions:

- Am I respected at work?

- Is my work and contribution valued?

- Am I empowered to take decisions at my work?

- Am I supported in trying to achieve and break boundaries of my performance?

- Am I given a fair treatment and opportunity to grow and learn

Nick: What is Toxic leadership?

Roy: It's a kind of leadership whereby a leader by his consistent arrogant behavior affects not only those who work with him but also takes away the trust and enthusiasm from the work environment. His effects are energy depleting, frustrating, a feeling of disrespect and ridicule.

Nick: Some of the characteristics of such Toxic Leaders are:

- Autocratic

- Practice a lot of prejudice and are often unfair in their judgement and play favorites.

- They are manipulative

- They are also intimidating

- They are rigid

- They create a strong inner circle of *yes men* sending wrong signals of what is valued in the organizations.

- They are obsessed by themselves, their vision and ideas. Inside they are actually like a stubborn child who only wants things his way.

- They often use fear to get done what they want, without understanding that it is people who take a company ahead. In an environment of fear, the culture of the company deteriorates leading to poor performance of the team and leading company to a downfall.

- Plays a lot of politics and blame games

- Does not pay much attention to the honest feedback of the customer and team

WHAT MAKES LEADERS SUCCEED & FAIL?

Leadership Ladder

Roy: Leadership is of different kinds, it could be supportive and constructive and it could be pseudo or toxic as well. A toxic leader may lead followers to destruction. For example Napoleon led himself & his followers to destruction. Though Napoleon had all the traits of leadership, except that he was driven by a personal ambition and not greater good of his followers and people of his country.

The leadership that is talked in this book is all about helpfulness, self-development & fair and just treatment.

Leadership in business environment has multifold challenges. It is:

- Not only to deliver results in today's competitive and challenging business environment, but also to prepare and anticipate future opportunities.

Nick: Since we have discussed about the leadership trait, is there a dark side of leadership? I mean are there some traits or behaviors of leaders because of which they fail along with their teams?

Roy: Leadership is a behavior as we have discussed earlier, as the leader slips in his behavior, his team's result changes. Leaders are highly productive individuals, leading their teams to achieve the goals envisioned.

However in their aspiration to be more competitive and achieve more they might have to pay a price in case they are:

- Missing on empathy

- Missing to develop team players and grooming more leaders

- Having lesser time to listen and connect with team members

- Focusing more on results and less on culture

- Not developing and investing to improve themselves

- Investing lesser time in engaging with employees and their morale

- By not being fair

- By favoring a few in the team

Nick: I am getting to understand, would that mean they get more into the numeric mode of an organizational performance and less in leading people role which brings their downfall?

Roy: Yes Nick!! It is the relationship with the team, their moral and commitment which lead to success. A leader is able to achieve continued success only if he continuously invests in people and stays connected with them ensuring they are engaged. The moment a leader shifts his focus to achieving only numbers he starts behaving like a manager. This additional push to perform without the supporting encouragement and empathy from the leader often leads to burn out the employees.

It is crucial that leaders must strike a balance keeping their team members' morale and engagement at the heart of the culture.

Nick: As leaders taste success along with their team, does that lead to inflated ego in them too?

Roy: Success may lead to arrogance among leaders if they are not constantly engaged in introspection!

Nick: I recall a quote from Socrates:

"To know is to know that you know nothing"

That is the meaning of true knowledge."

The real knowledge is about knowing that one does not know everything and that there is always more to learn. Learning is a continuous process and leveraging the strength of the team is an essential leadership trait. This trait is possible only when the leader has the realization that he needs to know more and stays humble

Roy: Do you know of some common faults leaders commit that leads to failure?

Nick: They may have a sense of having arrived after delivering a success. This feeling leads to complacency and may make them take things for granted.

Nick: They may get over ambitious in their targets or vision without investing in their team.

Roy: Leaders may also have a darker side to them which flashes when they are successful. They may become hungry for their personal growth, may get greedy to get more benefits and perks. These personal wants disconnect them from people and hence they start failing slowly and lose trust and influence.

Nick: Leaders may get rigid and loose agility and the quality to adapt.

Roy: In today's changing environment where businesses are being disrupted with revolutionary ways of solving problems, leaders must be agile in their approach to lead. However, not too many leaders have this capability to stay agile under stressed business conditions.

Sometimes under pressure leaders show some dark sides of their personalities.

The seven deadly sins and their opposing virtues are:

1. Pride – Humility

2. Avarice/Greed – Generosity

3. Envy – Love

4. Wrath/Anger – Kindness

5. Lust – Self Control

6. Gluttony – Faith and Temperance

7. Sloth – Zeal

Source: (Cooksey, 1995; Graham, 2000; Pyle, 1996).

Every day, a leader faces both personal and organizational challenges:

- Taking too long to recover from failure

- Not listening/ignoring the feedback

- Ignoring to build relationship based on trust

- They stop taking risks to keep growing.

- Real leaders don't take reckless decision based on what has always worked will work again.

- Get paralyzed by fear

- Poor self-management: taking care of themselves physically/emotionally/psychological and spiritually, i.e., Mind body and heart

- Leaders credibility or reputation suffers

- They are surrounded by yes man rather than those who provide innovation

- Ignoring the warning signs and doing nothing about them

- Lack of enthusiasm

- Taking leadership for granted: relying on knowledge without enterprise or having stopped serving post success

- Ambiguous expectations

- Lack of decision making or delayed decisions

Roy: Having an inflated ego is the biggest threat and barrier to leadership! Having an inflated ego is a big trap and very easy for leaders to get into that! As leaders achieve success, exceptional performance levels, recognition, respect and other perks makes it easier to fall in the ego trap! Leaders soon start believing that we are the smartest and the most effective resource in the organization. As they become egoistic they stop listening and they become so full of self that this attitude slowly isolates them from the team.

Though leaders must have a high self-esteem and confidence yet they should assume a collaborative role rather than an authoritative role. Ego encourages the belief that I am always right and blames others for any failure! Arrogant leaders refuse to listen to their team and force them to agree to their ideas even if not in the right direction.

Humility serves leadership Rick Warren once said,

"True humility is not thinking less of yourself; it is thinking of yourself less."

Richard Duane Warren is an American evangelical Christian pastor and author

Ego or individual recognition of neither the leader nor the follower should become a barrier in achieving

Nick: I did hear somewhere the full form of ego?

Edge God Out

"For those who exalt themselves will be humbled, and those who humble themselves will be exalted"

Christians read in Mathew 23:12

That is the beauty of this world that we can learn so much always from each other all the time. Inflated egos stop leaders to collaborate and learn from others. Ego also stops leaders to leverage the collaborative intelligence of the team, making it weak.

It also refers not to judge others & not bother about who is giving the idea or a suggestion based on his position in the team. As being a leader one should be open to accept best ideas and not get trapped into judging who is giving that suggestion. As being a leader one may easily fall prey to feeling superior and may miss out leveraging team intelligence and contribution.

Nick: But humility may be misinterpreted as a weakness

Roy: On the other hand humility is one of the biggest strength of the leaders

ESSENCE OF LEADERSHIP

"The superior leader gets things done with very little motion. He imparts instruction not through many words but through a few deeds. He keeps informed about everything but interferes hardly at all. He is a catalyst, and though things would not get done well if he weren't there, when they succeed he takes no credit. And because he takes no credit, credit never leaves him."

– Lao Tse, Tao TeChing

Was an ancient Chinese philosopher and writer. He is the reputed author of the Tao TeChing, the founder of philosophical Taoism

Nick: I am keen to know what the True Essence of leadership is.

Roy: There are famous lines by Warren Bennis

"No leader sets out to be a leader people set out to live their lives, expressing themselves fully. When that expression is of value, they become leaders so the point is not to become a leader. The point is to become yourself, to use yourself completely – all your skills, gifts and energies – in order to make your vision manifest. You must withhold nothing. You must in sum, become the person you started out to be and enjoy the process of becoming"

Warren Bennis has very beautifully captured the essence of leadership. He lays stress that true leaders don't aim to become leaders but during their lives they find themselves compelled to a purpose with all their commitment. It is actually a process of becoming and not proving to the world that they are leaders. It is a life process of what we become by chasing our calling, passion, purpose or a goal. It is during this pursuit of purpose which becomes higher than the leader himself that people discover their leadership skills.

ESSENCE OF LEADERSHIP

Roy: Leadership is complex and it cannot be learned as a skill it is in fact more an art form. It is something about expressing yourself.

Nick: What is the difference between expressing and becoming one's true self and not aiming to be an imitative leader or just a cosmetic leader!

Roy: You see if you join a new company as a senior most person, there is a pressure to prove oneself, so often such people start making big changes all around them so as to show they are there to make changes and make their presence felt in the organization. Their objective is more to show they are important

Nick: I have also observed that some people want to simply model certain leadership behavior. For example if a leader is stern and aims best in class quality and sometimes shows his serious displeasure to their team. Certain team members start to role model only that aspect feeling this works well so let's do that, however they do not know the entire perspective. The same leader is also connecting with the team on a day to day basis as well and truly cares for them

Nick: Leadership is not about being only analytical, data crunching, logical and technical issues. It is not limited to gauging individual performance only and yield and revenue management. There is more to leadership!

Roy: That is all about the left brain!

You can tell me more about the right brain as you are an artist yourself.

Nick: I can tell you about the right brain which is mostly about being artistic, creative, innovative and intuitive. But most of the organizations aim at analytical performance only and not being creative solution provider as that cannot be measured.

Roy: Very true the corporate culture is completely driven by the financial performance and not sustainable business development. The business owners are getting more and more influenced by instant results driven leadership.

Nick: In a way they are focusing on short term financial gains and not long term success. I see your point and I can substantiate that since I have been training and coaching students, professionals and organizations. Lot of left brain driven leaders are good at financial numbers and they don't care much about the company culture, customer or employee satisfaction, all they bother about is balance sheet.

Roy: Such organizations show higher employee attrition, lower employee morale and stress full work culture, decreasing customer loyalty, drop in the trust of the brand. But these signs don't show up in the balance sheets so it stays under cover. But soon it starts reflecting in the balance sheet as the company continuously loses its brand name, trust and quality. Hence a leader with a left and right brain serves better.

True business leader must be concerned not only about the revenue but other factors as well which drive the brand name, reputation & employee satisfaction, trust, quality and growth.

Nick: You are in way referring to being concerned and effectively working in achieving successful results in: financial balance sheet, people and society balance sheet. So would it also mean that leaders must be able to have qualities of left and right brain.

We may learn the most important leadership lesson from God! All around the globe people are in search of God! How is it that someone who created a perfect universe, nature making miracles happening everyday around us is not to be seen at all.

Yet the entire humanity worships this force in their own ways, and God on the other hand is not visible to take any credits. God keeps bestowing unlimited blessings on the humanity, always creating miracles without being seen around.

In a way it is like true and ultimate source of leadership, providing us all that we need to survive yet never there to take any credit while the entire world is in search of him

Leadership in a way is a reflection of this, true leaders are not self-serving but they serve others

LEAD LIKE A SHERPA

Roy: Let me explain leadership by example of a Sherpa!

Sherpa's are the leaders of mountain climbing expedition.

Nick: What is the key role of a Sherpa?

Roy: Just as a CEO is hired by an organization to lead the company to the best of heights similarly Sherpa's job is to lead the members of the expedition to the top of the mountain. Sherpa's are used to facing obstacles, dangerous snow covered unforeseen hindrances which they face with courage like a CEO who navigates business through a maze of choices and complex problems. The CEO tries to overcome the problem of complexities based on his expert judgement and experience, collaborates and leverages the competencies and strength of his team. The leader inspires and keeps the team motivated and energized towards achieving a common goal.

The behavior of Sherpa's truly represents the essence of a Leadership:

• To guide & inspire the team to the destination.

• To create a detailed plan and prepare for the expedition

• To face the challenges head on and chalk/carve a path for the team

• They are part of the team and work along with the team at all times, which develops respect, trust and strong relationships.

• Give them expert guidance, inspiration and push them to stretch and give their best

• Face difficult and life threatening circumstances, with grace, courage and grit which inspires confidence of the team.

They guide mountain expeditions in the face of huge challenges to stay ahead and take care of the entire expedition in all aspects, yet when the mountaineers reach the summit they feel they have achieved it. This is the power of leadership and the Sherpa's celebrate the victory with them

Nick: What are some of the leadership lessons that we can learn from Sherpa's?

Roy: Sherpa's are experts of their job, that is the reason the expedition members trust them with their lives. They not only have expert knowledge about the equipment, precautions and planning but are also expert climbers. So there walk and talk match.

Nick: That would mean that CEO not only knows what to do but also has a fair knowledge about the process of how to go about doing, executing and leading from the front.

Roy: And since they are climbers themselves they are in a position to understand the challenges a new climber would feel. They know clearly what their role is, it is not to climb the peak themselves only but to ensure that everyone reaches the top and returns back safe and sound as well. Since they always have this bigger picture in mind which is the safety of his expedition. Sometimes if there is extreme conditions on way they are humble enough to accept and call off the expedition keeping the safety of the team as the highest priority, only to be back another day when the weather conditions are better.

They aim one peak at a time; lead the expedition, making a way by clearing the obstacles and chalk out a safe path for the team

Nick: That is also very much like a CEO, who takes the risk to implement bold decisions and lead his team through the obstacles.

Roy: When the climbers reach the top, Sherpa's happily applaud the efforts of the climbers and celebrate their victory.

Nick: Which is all about sharing success credit and celebrating together?

Roy: True. One has to be patient while climbing; there is no way a Sherpa can play favorites to the climbers by giving extra attention to some and less to others. Everyone is treated similarly. Everyone carries there back pack themselves. No accepting of any personal favors or needs by Sherpa's, they are clear and firm to decline as they make sure it's a team expedition and everyone is sailing in the same boat. They create an environment of one team where everyone is treated equally and fairly.

Sherpa's by sheer nature of their work have built resilience

238 ❖ Leadership Plus

They are also calm and composed when facing a snow storm or a wild animal on the way.

Nick: They like a wise CEO show grace when they are faced with pressures and don't crumble. Sherpa's are very grounded and down to earth people. They mostly come from Nepal; they work extremely hard, and are cheerful with an almost infectious energy and are deeply connected family people.

Nick: I am amazed how much one can embody in leadership from Sherpa's

Roy:

"True leader like any Sherpa takes major responsibility of the expedition and take no credit for the success of it"

LEAD LIKE AN ORCHESTRA CONDUCTOR

Max Lucado Quotes. "A man who wants to lead the orchestra must turn his back towards the crowd."

– (Best selling Christian author: Anxious for Nothing)

Roy: I am sure you would love this one since you are a musician too and will have more to add since you know music more than me!!

Let us interpret what an orchestra conductor does? Let me ask you a set of questions?

Why is the orchestra Conductor standing with his back towards the audience?

Nick: Because his job is to conduct the concert as per the planned piece of music! And if he is facing the audience, the musicians would not be able to see and follow his directions thus the purpose of performing the concert will be defeated!

Roy: It also symbolic that effective leaders know how to keep themselves away from distractions and completely focus on their goals along with their team.

Nick: Orchestra conductor having his back towards the audience also signifies how leaders kind of stay immune to what the world is saying, reacting, criticizing, judging or applauding them. They are busy doing their job quietly and let the results to the talking. They focus on the team and their performance and not on the appreciation and adulation. This also keeps check on their egos as too much appreciation may make them arrogant.

Roy: Let us see what more can we learn here?

- Why is it that the orchestra conductor is on a little higher pedestal?

Nick: So that he can be visible to connect with his entire team and assist them all to play the concert with perfection. He is performing true to the purpose which is to completely ensure that the concert is performed in synergy of all musicians as planned

Roy: That reflects that a Leader like the orchestra conductor should be always available & approachable. Being visible to his team and at the same time working with them to achieve the goals together. Also it shows that his prime and only objective is to perform the task at hand which is to conduct the concert to perfection. He completely avoids out all distractions and so does his entire team, they all concentrate only on the notes they are playing till the performance is over.

By focusing on the musicians he kind of role models for every team member to not bother about the crowd but focus only giving their best and contribute to the symphony.

Nick: Let me add here, they all have a very clear plan and clearly defined role in the team for which they all have put in numerous hours of practice sessions together. Each musician is very clear about their role and performs their part to the best of their abilities as per the planned symphony.

It is very much like the CEO in an organization as he too clearly communicates the purpose, role, guidelines etc and once the team is trained and energized they are left to simply perform without being micro-managed. They also ensure that the work culture is in a way similar to as what is between the musicians. Similarly employees must feel confident, re-assured in their competencies and empowered to perform their tasks effortlessly without too much interference by the leaders. This leads to an accurate, flawless and expectation exceeding performance.

Roy: Nick you simply nailed that interpretation. So they have a plan in place, a clear vision, well planned, well-rehearsed and practiced flow, to ensure the entire orchestra is in sync with each other. Success of the performance depends on everyone, one error or one missed co-ordination can bring down the performance level drastically.

They have practiced a lot to work effectively as a team under the guidance of the orchestra conductor and look up to him for his expert advice to give their best performance

Roy: Since you are a musician, I have this question; is it be possible that some of the musicians playing in that concert are more talented than the leader and would be able to play all instruments more proficiently than him?

Nick: It is most likely that most of the musicians can play instruments better than the orchestra conductor.

What you mean here is that the orchestra conductor is more qualified and experienced as a leader to lead the team together. He understands the nuances of the different musicians and is well aware of the bigger vision to be achieved. He is the one who drives discipline, preparation and motivates the team to overcome mistakes. The Orchestra conductor inspires them to put in that extra effort beyond their limits to train and practice harder and play the piece effortlessly and flawlessly in the concert to achieve excellence

Roy: It also reflects that best leaders like the orchestra conductor develop more leaders by proper training, coaching and mentoring them to perfection

The orchestra conductor motivates his followers and team members to make them feel secure and confident in their own abilities, which leads to happy and relaxed faces while playing the orchestra live which adds to boosting their morale and confidence in front of the audience.

Nick: That is such an important aspect of leadership

Roy: What happens at the end of the concert?

Nick: As the concert ends and the audience starts clapping!

Roy: What is the reaction of the orchestra conductor as the audience claps?

Nick: He bows humbly to the audience and points out to the musicians highlighting by his gesture that it is they who performed so well thus deserve the applaud! So true leaders like the orchestra conductor share the credit of success and genuinely believe that they would have not been able to excel in isolation without the combined efforts of the team.

Roy: So a leader aims, at creating more leaders by serving them and are thrilled to see them succeed.

They are not hungry to steal the lime light of success rather are feel proud when the team outshines.

LEADERSHIP LESSON FROM THE LONGEST WINNING STREAK TEAM IN AMERICAN SPORT (151 GAMES WINNING STREAK)

We're not asking you to be perfect on every play. What we're asking of you and what you should be asking of each other is to give a perfect effort from snap to whistle."

– Coach Ladouceur

Ladouceur is the all-time longest winning streak test coach in California high school football and has led the De La Salle program to numerous championships. A film about his life was released on August 22, 2014, 'When the Game Stands Tall is a 2014 sports drama film'

Roy: "The Game Stands Tall" is a remarkable motion picture and inspiring true story of De La Salle High School Football team which broke all records for any American sport when they had a 151 game winning streak. In the movie Coach Bob Ladouceur gets a heart attack and the team loses tragically one of their star players. The team struggles and they lose their first game in years. It is a story about how Coach Bob inspires the team to make a comeback, based on values, integrity and faith

The story is about how giving a 100% effort is what a leader targets for, in the direction of their vision! Leaders set unachievable targets for themselves and at times they also expect extraordinary results as they very well aware that the team has a potential to do excel

Nick: How can leaders achieve a 100% Effort?

It is possible only when there are cordial relations and understanding within the team members, where egos and personal recognitions take a back seat as they can sabotage the entire team's effort.

Roy: Some of the best lessons to be learnt are: That the coach always aimed at inspiring the team members to give their best effort from the start whistle to the end whistle

It was not about being perfect at all times but giving their best effort at all times.

Nick: Which means?

Roy: The coach is more focused on achieving perfection in effort and not aiming at the highest score, which is the game changer! Not the end but the means, not only the result but the process day in day out. They are taught that there legacy is not about playing a good game one day, but how they have lived each day and moment with integrity, character, love, being responsible and being trust worthy to each other.

Focusing on the process is more important than the results as results are an outcome of well-defined processes only. The team objective is never to create a world record winning streak and within the team it is not discussed

---

"This program was founded on certain ideals – Perfection, Commitment, Compassion, Brotherhood, and Faith."

– Coach Ladouceur

Nick: Which means?

- The culture in the team is the key to how they feel and perform.

- That everyone in the team cares about each other like a family,

- The team is not only limited to performance or restricted to professional relationship but it extends to a kind of bonding as in a closely knit family.

Roy: It's a movie about how a coach trains a team to boldly face their fears yet stay humble during their victory. Coach trains them not only for the game but also how to lead their lives with integrity, character and courage. It tests the character of the team, it is not when everything is going right that a leader shines, but it is during the tough times when they are tested and deliver what they stand for. He constantly avoids any focus on the winning streak

Nick: I got a bucket full of learning.

There should be a sense of togetherness and genuine care amongst the team and the leader

Roy: **Which is not different than being in a family and at times best teams are as closely knit as families as they face together their fears, wins and losses! They celebrate their success**

together and stand for each other. All of this may sound too idealistic but it did work with record results for De La Salle.

The coach always laid stress on the fact that with great team bonding a team could defeat a team full of talent and stars too. **He had decoded and applied the fundamentals of team success, which was based on playing with dedication to and for each other and not letting each other down in performance**

Roy: Coach Bob focused on accountability, commitment and care for the fellow being. The coaching program of Bob Ladouceur aims at instilling the following into his team members: respect, love, commitment, character, discipline and accountability. Coach Bob always aimed at a higher purpose and not just winning. Winning was simply a by-product of the efforts put in by the team. He aimed at bringing out the best out of each one of his team to push them, to give their best. He saw football not only as a sport but as a ground to prepare his team for life. He emphasized that one life is defined by how one plays in the field. By learning to give 100% effort in the sports field one gets trained to give 100% in life too.

Nick: Would you share any practice which kept this high performance team together?

Roy: Coach Bob Lad practices a method of commitment card! He gives a card to each member of the team and they are supposed to write their commitment/goals for the coming week. For example to write a performance or a practice goal etc and this written commitment card would then be given to another player. After a week it was the job of the other player to speak about the other team member's performance, against the commitment made in all honesty and integrity.

Nick: So the commitment performance would be reviewed by a team member and not the coach. This would stress the point that we are also committed to each other and everyone's performance is interlinked, leading to an outstanding team effort.

Coach Bob works to inculcate in the team the commitment as he says:

"Don't let one another down"

Nick: I can't resist not sharing

The ultimate essence of leadership has been summed up in this shlokas from Shri Bhagwad Gita:

"KarmanyeVadhikaraste
Ma Phaleshu Kadachana,
Ma Karma Phala He tur Bhurma
TeySangostvaAkarmani"

Roy: It means "You have a right to "Karma" (actions) but never to any Fruits thereof. You should never be motivated by the results of your actions

Nick: Do your duty or 'karma' with full faith and devotion and be totally detached from its outcome. Don't work merely to reap the fruits and never let the result or 'phal' to overshadow your karma.(Phal is a word in hindi language, meaning the outcome of efforts)

In today's complex world entrepreneurs and leaders are getting desperate to achieve success that they often compromise work ethics and values. As they aim for short term gains looking for instant and outstanding results.

Leadership is a journey and not destination! Leaders and entrepreneurs enjoy challenges, clear obstacles, carve new paths and achieve new horizons. While they aim for the target they never forget to enjoy the journey. This attitude keeps them going and helps them see through troubled times as defeat and failure don't deter them.

THE IMPORTANCE OF UN-REASONABLE LEADER

The reasonable man adapts himself as per the world; the unreasonable one persists in trying to adapt the world to him, therefore, all progress depends on the unreasonable man."

– George Bernard Shaw was an Irish playwright, critic, polemicist and political activist

Nick: Isn't being unreasonable a negative expression?

And should it not be avoided in corporate world?

Roy: By being unreasonable does not mean harsh or I don't care attitude! One of the key reasons why leaders succeed is that they challenge the status quo and look for innovation leading to extra ordinary results. Changing means leaving one's comfort zone which is hard. They are driven by their purpose, thus are often ridiculed but they believe that it is possible. Leaders are often viewed as unreasonable which is based on leaders trust on his team to stretch and achieve more.

Nick: You mean it's a gap, between how a leader thinks and how a team member views their own performance potential. Leaders know that the team has the potential to stretch and achieve more, however the team sometimes doesn't have that level of trust on themselves. And it is a leader's job to develop that confidence and trust within the team members to believe that these seemingly unreasonable targets are very much a reality

Let me ask you a question, wasn't writing this book itself an unreasonable uphill task in itself?

Nick: Well with you around it has been a lot of self-discovery of leadership and learning journey and yes it has been lot of work

Leaders see in others what others can't see in them. They are the lions who inspire a culture of courage.

Roy: Leaders continuously challenge themselves to live a life in the stretch zone! They continue to improve their own as well as the skills of their team. They have unreasonable expectations from themselves physically, emotionally and intellectually. This attitude pushes innovation and out of the box thinking. They ensure that their team stays away from just being mediocre, complacent or too comfortable. They aim to accomplish the vision. They continuously inspire their team so that they can achieve the vision they have thought of. The world is full of people who make an excuse and fizzle out half way through a project blaming others for the failure. – I am too busy

- I don't have a sufficient team

- I am doing my best as I can, yet it seems impossible

- I am not getting the co-ordination required to complete the task

- The competition is certainly better than us and there is no way we can win

- We don't have the required resources

- Some people will always find an excuse for not doing what is required to be done.

Leaders ensure that they and their team stay away from behaving this way. Leaders by getting a little pushy get tasks done which seem otherwise uphill and impossible. They have self-belief and faith in their team which ensures that the objective is achieved.

Nick: I understand the positive side of the demanding leaders! Walt Disney's concept of creating Disneyland was rejected over 300 times before it got financed, KFC (Kentucky Fried Chicken) founder Colonel Sanders was rejected over a 1000 times before finding any takers for his recipe.

Leaders not only have out of the box expectations from self but they inspire the others as well to outperform their own expectations from themselves.

WHY LEADERS MUST BE GOOD FOLLOWERS

Best Followers Make The Best Leaders

Roy: It is so much a fad that everyone wants to be a leader as if being a follower was not important. Leadership is a behavior; it has nothing to do with the title. Nothing worthwhile can be achieved alone. All the big movements have been achieved with combined efforts of the team. The leaders emerge out of the followers only.

The face is however a leader who was also once a follower.

"He who cannot be a good follower cannot be a good leader."

– Aristotle

"Being a good follower does not make you a sheep!"

Roy: What one learns by being a good follower is what helps them shape into good leader.

Nick: What does one learns being a good follower?

Roy: One learns the following traits being a follower:

- Understanding how a team works and collaborate for producing great results.

- They know how customers, colleagues feel and behave during different situations.

- They also get to observe the traits of the good and bad followers and hence can easily identify the bad ones when they turn leaders.

- Good followers are extremely committed positively driven and aligned to the vision or the goal of the enterprise.

- They have a solution driven approach and take ownership of the project that they are a part of.

In fact in a lot of ways the qualities that a leader looks in a follower are at times similar to the qualities a follower looks in a leader.

Nick: Allow me to share some qualities that are similar between leaders and followers:

For example good followers are:

- Committed to the purpose and contribute their best and do not give lame excuses or play the blame game

- Are happy and comfortable to collaborate just like leaders and succeed together

- Are happy to see others succeed and grow just like leaders

- Are humble and know they need to constantly get better, keep learning and aim to excel

- Seek help from their fellow colleagues

- They can be trusted and stay accounted for

- Extend a helping hand to the new ones who come onboard in the team

LEADERSHIP MUST BE AUTHENTIC & CREDIBLE

"I realised the shoes I had to fill were far too big to mimic (taking over from his uncle J. R. D. Tata in 1991), and so I decided to be myself and that to do what I thought was right would be the way to go."

– Ratan Tata

Nick: Why is there a scarcity of authentic leaders in today's world?

Roy: There is so much pressure on today's generation to succeed that often young leaders target to get ahead and aim only money, position and fame. In that process they miss out on discovering self.

Authentic leaders are those who are genuine and not behaving as a leader because they have a certain title which is cosmetic leadership. Authentic leaders show how they feel about their colleagues and are transparent. They are not afraid to hide their true personality as a person which develops higher trust and loyalty among the followers. An authentic leader is aware of his strengths and weaknesses, delegates' authority and extends support to his team. He is not afraid to accept his mistakes and shortcomings and hence comes across as a fair person developing strong relationships and trust.

Authentic leaders are not worried about showing their vulnerable side. People trust you when you are yourself i.e. genuine, sincere and transparent in your everyday behavior.

Nick: Does that mean Leaders equipped with better strategy and vision will fail if they are not able to instill trust in their team?

Trust forms the core of the leadership, people easily identify a fake leader.

Roy: It is about walking the talk, showing passion and expertise in the job and striking a chord of trust with the team. A leader is respected and followed when he displays strong character and integrity which drives his behavior. One cannot be pseudo as a leader and still be trusted, as people can easily see through a fake behavior. To be trusted one must be real, should have genuine, care and compassion for his team. With all these characteristics at place the team is happy to align themselves with the goals and objectives as per the leader's vision.

Nick: Can you share any example of an authentic leader?

Roy: One of the most authentic leaders is Mr. Ratan Tata.

TATA Group of companies is known for their ethics, values and principles and is respected for that worldwide. TATA is an house hold cult brand name known for its principles and integrity. TATA business empires is based on ethical business practices, managing with transparency, and staying responsible to society and employees and stakeholders. The company is known for not compromising on its values and principles. Mr. Ratan Tata by living the principles in his day to day work life has inspired and inculcated a culture in his business empire which is based on trust, integrity & transparency. I have read the concept of triple balance sheet that Ratan Tata demonstrates.

Nick: I have heard of financial balance sheet? What is triple balance sheet?

Roy: The three balance sheet business management is

Financial Balance Sheet: refers to the traditional financial performance of the company

People Balance Sheet: refers to how a company connects and behave with the people in the company, its customers and others

Planet Balance Sheet: refers to how responsible is the company behavior with regard to the society and the planet earth.

Ratan Tata is a classic example and a role model of authentic and inspiring leadership. In my opinion he is the finest leader, whose inner values and outer behavior are integrated. This walk the talk behavior is the hallmark of authentic leaders, leading to trust and inspiring the value based culture in the entire business group. No wonder TATA group has employees who work in an environment which is based on trust, compassion, transparency and faith on the leadership and its vision.

Nick: Allow me to quote a small example from Infosys! Once Narayan Murthy, Chairman Infosys, during the initial days of business set up refused to pay bribe to a telephone company whereby they had to wait for a year to get the telephone connection.

For example Howard Schultz closed 8000 stores in 2018 for racial sensitivity training for approximately 175000 employees. Starbucks in India has a JV with TATA's and is the first QSR to provide 5 working days a week for their staff.

Roy: What is a QSR?

Nick: Quick service restaurants, smirks! Love it when I know something's more than you!!!

LEAD LIKE A SAMURAI

Himanshu Kaushal

Samurai means: "the one who serves "and is referred to those who are of noble birth and guard to secure. Bushido refers to "the way of warriors"" is a collective term used in Japan which refers to the code of conduct of samurai

Nick: What is that we can learn from a Samurai mindset?

Roy: They fight to win and not just there to fight.

That means committing 100% to the target, by doing the best possible skill preparation, physically, mentally and emotionally. They win the battle in their mind before going to the battle.

Lord of Echigo in the 16th century explained the Samurai's fatalistic approach to combat:

"Fate is in Heaven, the armour is on the breast, success is with the legs. Go to the battlefield firmly confident of victory, and you will come home with no wounds whatever.

"Engage in combat fully determined to die and you will be alive; wish to survive in the battle and you will surely meet death. When you leave the house determined not to see it again you will come home safely; when you have any thought of returning you will not return.

"You may not be in the wrong to think that the world is always subject to change, but the warrior must not entertain this way of thinking, for his fate is always determined."

A Samurai does not go to a battle with the mind-set of being safe but a mind-set of winning the battle. He is not focused on returning safely but fighting a fierce battle. By focusing on safety he may not be able to give his 100% in the battle which could be a fatal mistake. Safety concerns will give him conflicting thoughts to fight or to be safe or fight to win. These conflicting thoughts take away the courage and the complete effort to win. Any thought of returning home will only create a deviation in mind rather makes a divided effort thus making them less of a fighter.

Nick: In order to achieve that they must have undivided attention in the fight, to strike when required and defend when needed.

Roy: All the training and discipline are of no use if that cannot be translated into performance.

They must have unwavering belief to win. Developing a mental strength and belief in self where there is no doubt in the mind of a Samurai could be the difference between life and death.

Samurai's are fiercely committed to their task, in-fact they are ready to die for the sake of that. "Honour" is what they live for, and their word is their promise.

Nick: It also also refers to, that we must win the battles within us before we go out to become victorious in the real battlefield.

Sun Tzu writes:

"Victorious warriors win first and then go to war, while defeated warriors go to war first and then seek to win."

Roy: That would mean they must have a certain belief that they are going to win in the battlefield. They do not approach the battlefield with the mindset to see how it goes. This attitude is not a positive attitude and will never win battles! Same are life battles!

Lots of people just move ahead without any conviction and mental strength, and when they meet any roadblocks they simply give up and accept defeat. Similarly organizations that are at the top spot do not go half-heartedly towards innovation or moving into new paths they put it in 100% of their efforts to achieve the purpose.

Here are Bushido's Eight Virtues as explicated by NitobeInzo, in the book Bushido: The Soul of Japan. The Boschido code refers not only to the professional but personal code of conduct as well. It is an unwritten code of conduct which is based on the 8 principles

RECTITUDE & JUSTICE	HEROIC COURAGE
Is about the morally correct behaviour, being fair, doing the right thing, taking fair decisions, being loyal	Courage is counted as a virtue only when it is used for doing the right thing

SINCERE	BENEVOLENCE, COMPASSION
Samurai exercise sincerity in every virtue in all their behaviour	The key requirement in leaders is to have following traits love, affection, sympathy & magnanimity

HONOUR	Politeness
Sense of Self-esteem, Self-Worth Dignity	Behaviour out of Courtesy & good manners that are respected

LOYALTY	CHARACTER & SELF CONTROL
Samurai warriors stay fiercely loyal to those they have commitment to. Their word is as good as promise	Control over impulsive behaviour. Controlling false pride, greed anger etc

LEADERSHIP LESSONS FROM SAMURAI

Roy: I will be sharing some quotes which are relevant even after centuries by Miyamoto Musashi, (The Book of Five Rings) and you may try to interpret them

(Miyamoto Musashi, also known as Shinmen Takezō, Miyamoto Bennosuke or, by his Buddhist name, Niten Dōraku, was a

Japanese swordsman, philosopher, strategist, writer with an undefeated record in his 61 duels

Nick: Let us start.

Roy: Some of his quotes have priceless lessons for leadership

---

"You must understand there is more than one path to the top of the mountain." (Miyamoto Musashi)

Nick: Which means there are more than one solution to a problem!

Roy: "You can only fight the way you practice" (Miyamoto Musashi)

Nick: This means that a team must invest time regularly on continuous learning, as their performance is based on how hard they train.

Roy: "Do nothing which is of no Use" (Miyamoto Musashi)

Nick: This refers to being completely focused on the vision and not getting distracted or deviated. This also means that one should stay highly productive and focus on the most vital and effective aspects to achieve the best. It also implies not to indulge in wasteful activities which are not directed towards the goal progression.

Roy: "I choose to live by choice not by chance" (Miyamoto Musashi)

Nick: It refers to living a life of design not a life of default

Roy: "If you wish to control others you must first control yourself" (Miyamoto Musashi)

Nick: This refers to Personal Leadership, which includes being disciplined, practicing self-control, developing skills and working hard.

Roy: "Think lightly of yourself and deeply of the world"

(Miyamoto Musashi)

Nick: Staying humble and not having an inflated ego despite having power and numerous other achievements. As false pride is a sure path to downfall. One must stay humble and polite and feel light without any status baggage weight to move ahead faster.

Roy: "All men are the same except for their belief in their own selves, regardless of what other may think of them"(Miyamoto Musashi)

Nick: It is finally about self-confidence and self-belief which is the differentiating factor between people with commitment, discipline and self-control one can raise self in all areas.

Roy: "Do not regret what you have done" (Miyamoto Musashi)

Nick: Do not spend time over failures learn a lesson and move ahead. Failed attempts should not be taken to heart.

Also one should not waste time over analyzing past failures which may lower one's confidence and morale.

Roy: "The only reason a warrior is alive is to fight and the only reason a warrior fights is to win" (Miyamoto Musashi)

Nick: Once a goal is set one should not deviate from it. It refers to being completely decisive and putting in everything to achieve it. It should not be half-hearted attempt. Half-hearted decisions and casual efforts don't give results.

Roy: Be calm believe and have faith!

Nick: Why do I get the feeling that with Samurai discussion you have almost summed up our entire journey of leadership?

Roy: May be we have covered the journey, but it is not about knowing it, it is all about doing and practicing what we have learned. Most of us do not leverage our talent. Dreams must be realized, and should not remain mere fragmented imagination. It is not about thinking only but taking big action towards our future, facing our fears, overcoming failures and obstacles. Fuel the pull of the future objectives rather than getting pulled down by negative influences and bad habits or indiscipline.

Nick: Paying the mild painful price of discipline so that we don't have to pay a mega price of failure.

Roy: Learn one lesson from the clock, which is that the needles of the clock always are on the move. So take big action consistently and keep moving.

Nick: The ratio of hard work vs rest is also explained in bible. "Six days you shall labor, but on the seventh day you shall rest; even during the plowing season and harvest you must rest. Exodus 34:21

Nick: I can't help sharing a quote from Roger Federer

Roy: I was expecting that all the way a quote from your favourite sports personality.

"It is always in my mind still that I can crush anybody. That's not an issue. But I think that is the same for most athletes. If you don't believe you can win tournaments anymore, then you can't do it."

– Roger Federer

Roger Federer is often referred to as G.O.A.T Greatest of All Time (Tennis)

Like legendary sports names, musicians, business man, Sherpa's and the Samurai's, legendary companies and leaders practice the same.

They give 100% commitment to the purpose, take more risks, show courage to innovate, tread new paths, trust and share power and credit of success! They aim at providing an environment fueled with trust, responsibility and empowerment which grow more leaders.

Nick: They aim at unleashing The Leader With-in us

Thank you to all unsung leaders who tirelessly and consistently continue to inspire those who need. Sometimes

- With a timely gentle push

- Inspiring by being a role model

- With a kind word of encouragement and guidance

- With a stick of discipline

- By inspiring them to achieve extraordinary achievements.

Lead-Succeed-Win

ABOUT THE AUTHOR

Neeraj Chandhok is an acclaimed author, academician, corporate trainer, business consultant & an entrepreneur. After years of experience of teaching, training and research, Mr. Chandhok got convinced that leadership and serving attitude is essential component for success in personal and professional life.

Author of: "Customer Plus" – Staying Competitive in the Age of Customer Service

www.neerajchandhok.com